BACKSTAGE
WHO DOES WHAT IN THE THEATRE

Judith Cook

HARRAP
London

First published in Great Britain 1987
by HARRAP Ltd
19-23 Ludgate Hill, London EC4M 7PD

ISBN 0–245–54532–8

Phototypeset by Falcon Graphic Art Ltd
Wallington, Surrey

Printed and bound in Great Britain by
Mackays of Chatham Limited

Contents

Acknowledgments   4

Preface   5

CHAPTER 1   The Stage Manager's Tale   7

CHAPTER 2   The Production Manager's Tale   15

CHAPTER 3   The Casting Director's Tale   23

CHAPTER 4   The Designer's Tale   29

CHAPTER 5   The Property Maker's Tale   37

CHAPTER 6   The Wardrobe Mistress's Tale   47

CHAPTER 7   The Make-Up Artist's Tale   55

CHAPTER 8   The Dresser's Tale   63

CHAPTER 9   The Sound Man's Tale   67

CHAPTER 10   The Lighting Designer's Tale   77

CHAPTER 11   The Voice Teacher's Tale   83

CHAPTER 12   The Composer's Tale   89

CHAPTER 13   The Fight Director's Tale   97

CHAPTER 14   The Dance Director's Tale   105

and

A Profile of the Crucible Theatre, Sheffield   109

Acknowledgments

I would like to thank all the people interviewed in this book for giving up their time to the project. Also the staff of the National Theatre, Royal Shakespeare Company and the Crucible Theatre, Sheffield, for all their help.

Picture credits

Donald Cooper (by permission of the RSC), p.6; Ivan Kyncl (by permission of the RSC), p.14; Reg Wilson (by permission of the RSC), p.28; Samuel Teicher, p.82; Joe Cocks Studio, p.88; *Mail on Sunday, You Magazine*, p.96; John Haynes, p.104; Simon Cook, pp. 22, 36, 46, 54, 62, 66, 76.

All the pictures in the Crucible section were taken by Gerry Murray.

Preface

When you go to the theatre the performance that you see is the result of the work of a great many people of whom the actors are only the most obvious. Behind the scenes are all those who have co-operated to the best of their ability in making the show a success.

There are numerous books about and by actors and directors. This is an attempt to look at some of those who work behind the scenes, told, as far as possible, in their own words.

For this I have gone to those who are known to be good at their jobs: some work for one or other of the great national companies, the Royal Shakespeare Company and the National Theatre, some are freelance.

But I thought it also interesting to look at how those same jobs, and others, are undertaken in the smaller enclosed world of a regional repertory company and I chose the Crucible Theatre in Sheffield for this section of the book.

The aim is to inform those who would like to know a little more about what goes into a performance and possibly to interest others who might be thinking of making a non-acting career in the theatre.

These interviews took place between February 1985 and June 1986. Since then, it is of course possible that some of those who talked to me have moved on.

Judith Cook NEWLYN 1986

Frances Barber (Ophelia) and Roger Rees (Hamlet) in the RSC's 1984 Stratford
production of *Hamlet*.

The Stage Manager's Tale

1 Sonja Dosanjh started in stage management at the age of eighteen as a student with the Cambridge Theatre Company. 'It was sheer luck. I was in the right place at the right time. I developed an interest in stage management at school. I went to a girls' Convent which didn't really believe in drama at all but when you were about thirteen you had to perform in a play. The sister in charge went down the rows of desks and you were just told what part you were to play — no auditions or readings or anything like that. I remember we did *The Emperor and the Nightingale*, but by the time she got to me she had run out of acting parts so I was told to be stage manager. I had no idea what she meant or what the job was about. So I read some books and did it and I loved it.

'I spent the rest of my school-days studying during the day and rushing off to the Arts Theatre in Cambridge at night doing anything I could — front of house, dressing, helping with stage electrics. They let me do it because they could see I was so interested. I remember one time ironing shirts for the Royal Ballet (who were touring) at lunchtime and then rushing back to study in the afternoon.

'So I got to know the people involved in the Cambridge Theatre Company really well and they saw I was quite serious about wanting a career in stage management. I had thought I would go to drama school and take a course but I was very lucky because they said "why not come and be a student assistant stage manager here?" so I did. I spent two-and-a-half years just learning actually on the job both at the theatre and touring all around England. It's very demanding, touring.

'You get a bit of free time during the day but most of your week is taken with getting there, unpacking and getting the show on; and before you know where you are then you're taking it all down again, packing it up and going on to the next venue. Then all kinds of things can happen. I've had to trace lost parcels, skips and pieces of scenery and we've even lost actors and actresses. We had one show, for instance, where some of the cast could commute and one actress who was commuting every day was on a train when it broke down. She got off in the middle of nowhere, tramped across fields, dialled 999 from the nearest call-box and the police rushed her into Southampton where she just made it by curtain up. . . .

'I stayed with the Cambridge Theatre Company for two-and-a-half years by which time I was able to see what other opportunities there were in both the technical and the administrative side of working in the theatre and I decided I would most like to be a company manager. Over the years I just worked my way up the ladder from being an assistant stage manager to a deputy and finally to a stage manager, working for different companies. I did a West End theatre, I did Rep, I worked at the Belgrade Theatre in Coventry, I worked for the BBC and I toured abroad. I had a wonderful cross section of experience in all sorts of aspects of theatre. Then I went to the Oxford Playhouse as joint stage and company manager which was the very first time I achieved the company manager role and I loved it, particularly when we went on tour.

'I came to Stratford and the Royal Shakespeare Theatre four years ago as company manager although that meant I had to drop the stage management side. I do miss it but I have a lovely job and it's a very special place to work, with a fine group of actors, lots of problems but plenty of support. You never know what the day is going to throw at you especially during technical rehearsals. I sit up in the stalls in case anybody has any problems and watch the stage manager up there running the rehearsal, that is running the technical side of it, and I think sometimes: "Oh, I'd love to do that again."

'My responsibilities are to the acting company and to stage management. I am first base for all their problems. First let's take the actors. I sort out contractual difficulties (anything I can't deal with I take to the casting director), their rehearsal problems, their wages right through to their domestic worries. We have a company of about sixty actors and ten stage management every year and we guarantee to provide them with housing. You get people who want a bedsit or those who want a five-bedroomed house because they are bringing the kids, the nanny and a couple of dogs and some chickens. Even when you've got them in their accommodation it doesn't stop there. They always seem to be locking themselves out so I keep a set of duplicate keys. . . .

'We get the rare ones who have breakdowns. I spend a fair bit of time in the hospital, mainly in casualty. I'm forever taking actors who have had bits of their fingers sliced off in sword fights or have damaged their knees. Thank God I've never had anything serious. I suppose I'm a social worker, a welfare worker, a mother to them and I deal with any problems caused by their being away from home. It's a six-day week contract up here and a lot of them don't get home that often so they need their families to come here and see them if they are not here already. Because of separation, too, you can have relationships breaking up.

'We do work them terribly hard. There are a few people who are only in one production and that is relatively easy from the work point of view, but it is slightly difficult in another because if their play doesn't play that often in the repertoire they feel cut off from the rest of the company. But most of the actors are in four out of five or five out of six plays and they work from 10.30 in the morning often until after 11.30 at night. There are considerable pressures here.

'The other side of my work is looking at practical rehearsal problems, the scheduling of rehearsals, booking of rehearsal rooms, the hiring and firing of stage management. Take the situation now which is a typical one. We've got all the Stratford season plays on and you would think it would be easy, except that in a week, on Monday, we start rehearsing another show in London so I'll have to spend half of my week there looking after a new company. It's a revival but there are few people in it from the first production — it's mainly a new company.

'So we rehearse for nine weeks in a church hall at Waterloo which I've had to book and organize. Within three weeks again we start rehearsing another play for the Barbican. Two weeks after that there's a children's play with a cast of five which is going to be done at The Other Place in Stratford over Christmas. Come the end of January we start all over again and begin rehearsing for the new Stratford season, although at this stage (mid-autumn) we don't know yet what plays are going into the repertoire next year. The forward planning sometimes leave a little to be desired. . . . It'a a great shame, the one big frustration of the job.

'You might think it should be very easy to know in Stratford what Shakespeares you are going to be doing next year because there are only thirty-seven plays and you've got to have a balanced season, but it's very difficult to get many leading actors to sign themselves up for a year too far in advance in case a film or something better comes up. It is also very difficult for us because all our work from Stratford transfers to the Barbican and the availability of directors can be very difficult to work around. If they are not directing something in Stratford they may well be opening something in London, and it is hard to schedule the existing actors into any new work you might be doing in London because suddenly you find some people's contracts end at different times and they might not want to stay. It depends a lot on the offers we can make them.

'It's a real Catch 22 and it makes scheduling very difficult. I'm not involved in the actual planning, but as soon as we know what is happening then my job is to make other people's decisions happen. For instance, I know we will have to rehearse the regular Stratford season from early in the New Year so I assume I'm going to be rehearsing two or three productions at once in London during January and February; therefore I've already booked rooms for those rehearsals hoping I've not under- or over-booked. We have tremendous problems in London with rehearsal space. We lost our

9

rooms in Floral Street. The Barbican has two rooms but they are naturally used by the Barbican company and they are not even enough to take all the Barbican work. So it means church halls and whatever we can get, any old space. Because of the size of the shows we very rarely need only a small room. For *Nicholas Nickleby*, for instance, I had a brief to look around for somewhere at least sixty feet by sixty and there are very few places that size available where you can put up a scaffolding rehearsal set. Finally we found an old church on the Waterloo roundabout.'

What makes a good stage manager? I inquired.

'I think you have to be very stable. You need a terrific sense of humour and you've got to have plenty of common sense. Common sense is the greatest gift you can have in stage management. You also have to be a sympathetic person but strong with it.

'With the RSC you do have a tremendous back-up as it's such a large organization — you've a Props Department, wigs, wardrobe, all the workshops in the main house. The people working in The Other Place do get a certain amount of that kind of back-up but it's actually no bad thing for stage management there to have to beg, borrow and steal props. It's a real contrast from the main house. In Oxford, for instance, stage management was much more involved in the getting and making of props and buying them with the designers. Here in Stratford, main house stage management will only provide rehearsal props. All the real ones are made in the Prop Shop or are bought by a member of that department with the designer.

'Whereas in The Other Place it's much more like a small Rep company and I think it's very good for stage management to have to work that way. I'm the one in overall charge of all of it, actors and stage management, whether they are performing in a tent, down a railway line or out in the streets like when we did *The Dillen*. The stage management on that was wonderful; they were the most sensible people but it was a nightmare keeping track of over a hundred in the cast and hundreds and hundreds and hundreds of props.

'Obviously the worst time when things can go wrong and you have to make instant decisions is during an actual performance. If it happens during the day or in rehearsals that's fairly easily solved but stage management is an extremely responsible occupation.

'The stage manager is in overall charge and sits in the box and oversees it all, especially at the crucial technical rehearsals which are very much for stage management, but it is the deputy stage manager who is really in the hot seat. If there is an error by the DSM it can cause absolute chaos. If, say, they bring in a 'flying' piece too early while there is still an actor on stage and before the piece of scenery on

10

a truck has been struck, the result can be a complete shambles. You have to have split-second timing and you only need to be a tiny bit out for it to turn into a nightmare.

'Obviously there are always problems dealing with stage crews and even the best of them can make mistakes, but if you are with a touring company in a different place each week with a different stage crew then those problems just multiply. Monday nights are always very hairy.

'But for all deputy stage managers there are constant problems. Some are comparatively simple, but frightful if you get them wrong. There's nothing worse than pressing the button expecting bird song and getting the sound of a steam engine. . . . The DSM sits in at all rehearsals all the way through. He or she keeps a prompt copy which contains all the actors' moves. When the stage of the technical rehearsals is reached he then has to add in all the lighting cues — and it's possible to have three or four hundred lighting cues — sound cues, all the flying cues, music cues, actors' entrances and exits, trap cues, traps coming up from below, smoke guns, just everything that happens on stage is cued by the deputy stage manager. Nobody can do anything without a cue and the system of cues is a red and a green light. The DSM has a board with a row of red lights and a row of green, marked "flies", "sound", "electrics", etc. Your red light is "warn" and your green "go" and they are all linked up to the various bits of the theatre, and as soon as you see your green light you do whatever your next cue is. So you see why the DSM is always in the hot seat. During the performance the stage manager is simply a support. It's a very hard job and often with our shows, which are big and complex, the DSM's prompt copy looks extraordinary — you can hardly see any text at all.

'It's very rare that only one thing happens at once. More often there is a sequence where the music starts, lights change, a flying piece goes out, then some trucks move on, lights change again, there is some smoke. You have to keep to split-second timing to give them the right cues.

'The most basic job is that of assistant stage manager, the ASM. He's mainly responsible for the props, making sure everything is exactly on place on stage and that props which are not on stage are in the right place when the actor wants them.

'But with the best will in the world and however hard you try, things can go wrong. We had a wonderful set here for *Hamlet* recently. The stage was raked and it split open to make the grave. There was a classic night when they all trooped on with the dead Ophelia on a litter and would you believe it something went wrong with the electronics and the grave jammed. There wasn't enough space for anybody to get into it. So they hung on to Ophelia through the whole scene betwen Hamlet and Laertes and the rest; then it all ground to a halt and Claudius said: "Ah, now we'll bear Ophelia back to the chapel!" They'd come all the way out to bury her and then they had to carry her back again. I don't think the audience really noticed it but some of them must have thought it was a bit odd to carry her out and say all that about burying her just to take her back again, but it's amazing what you can get away with — murder sometimes. You can see why the job of DSM is so very highly stressed. It is both emotionally and physically demanding and all the pressure is on you from the moment that you say "house lights out". You're running the show. If an actor forgets a line or a bit of business or something happens like Ophelia's grave being too small for the body, then it often affects all the next cues so you have to be constantly on the ball.

'We prompt verbally here. We usually only get a couple, often well into the season and for no particular reason. In Shakespeare, though, experienced actors can often keep themselves going somehow until they remember the right words.

'I think the very worst thing that ever happened to me was in Oxford. We had a very complicated set for *Peer Gynt*, when we had to go straight from the storm scene into the mad scene. The storm had a huge piece of grey silk which came down from the flies horizontally and then was pulled vertical. On this particular night it completely and utterly fouled up on the lights and ripped, and half of it was hanging and the other half was in heaps on the floor. The mad people's cage had to come in at the same time and there was just an almighty tangle in the flies. You could see everything come in all caught up and the cage was about to crash down on to the heads of the actors already on stage. . . .

'We started off by kind of whispered shouts which had no effect then we bawled out "Run" and finally the stage management staff had to run on and literally shove the actors out of the way as the whole lot crashed down on stage. There was no hope of just going on with the performance, it was in such a tangle and such a mess. We had to explain to the audience, stop the show, clear it all up and then carry on as best we could.'

Possibly her oddest experience was the day a large square parcel was delivered to the RSC. When they opened it the smell nearly knocked them out. Someone had kindly arranged to leave their skull to the RSC for use in *Hamlet* and it had not been properly treated. . . . 'We tried hanging it out on a line at the back of the prop shop but it just kept on smelling . . . we gave up in the end.'

12

How do others in the theatre regard stage management?

'If something goes wrong for an actor the first person he sees when he comes off is the stage manager, so often it is the stage manager who gets it all — it's the frustration. You know it isn't really directed at you personally, it's just that the actor has had a bad time.

'I have found most directors relatively easy to work with. These days they are far more aware of stage management problems. I've been in the theatre now for ten years and when I started it was unusual for women to want to make a career in stage management. It wasn't considered a proper career. You were almost a servant, the dogsbody who swept the stage and made the tea and there was usually only one of you. It is only in the last five or six years that it has become properly recognized as a profession and it is realized how skilled you have to be. Also over the last ten years shows have become much more complicated and far more technical. Design standards are much higher, computers are used much more in lighting and sound, so it is more recognized that it is a highly skilled profession.

'I think most directors now working in theatre with the kind of equipment that they do have to work with rely very heavily on stage management and I think they do appreciate good stage management and just what we are being asked to do. They are very rarely unreasonable any more — at least not *very* unreasonable!

'Our aim is not to be noticed. It's good that as a member of the audience you can go to the theatre and all you see is what is on stage. You shouldn't have to worry about anything else, about what's gone on to get it there. You don't have to think how many hours went in to getting it all right. You should just be able to sit and watch a good, smooth-running show.'

The RSC's production of *A Midsummer-Night's Dream* 1986. Paul Venables (left) as Flute; Pete Postlethwaite (right) as Bottom; with Donald McBride (behind) as Snout.

The Production Manager's Tale

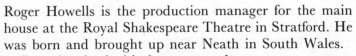

2 Roger Howells is the production manager for the main house at the Royal Shakespeare Theatre in Stratford. He was born and brought up near Neath in South Wales.

'I was involved with the amateur theatre at an extremely early age because my family, my father particularly, were very keen amateur actor/directors, so I used to go along and do it. In South Wales there is a very strong amateur tradition. I used to go along to all the rehearsals but I was incredibly shy and wouldn't perform. I only realized I enjoyed doing it at the advanced age of seventeen in a school production when they wanted a lot of walk-on people and these were recruited from the sixth form. That seemed quite fun because I knew a lot of people there and there was no great strain involved because none of us were saying anything, and so I did a walk-on in *Caesar and Cleopatra*. Then somebody dropped out from a small part of about twelve lines and I went in and did that and it wasn't half as embarrassing as I thought it would be.

'From that moment on I became involved in the amateur theatre and I always did a lot of everything — acting, directing, stage managing — because they used to do something, even if only a one-act play, every week. It was great fun because you did it all yourself: if you were stage manager you sort of cobbled the scenery together and you painted things and you made costumes. So you did a bit of everything, although not necessarily at the same time. We helped each other out and there was a very strong junior section, people about my own age, who happened to come together at the same time and were all very keen. One other thing also is that when you did these weekly productions it was the accepted thing that it was free. It was open house from a criticism point of view so you could get up and criticize, and the director, or the producer as we called him in those days, would sit on stage and respond and it was great fun with a real family atmosphere. There were a lot of families involved, both parents and children.

'There was a lot more theatre around in those days than people think too. As I have said, my father was a very keen theatre-goer. When we were on holiday we used to go to London for a week and see a week full of plays, two on the days when there was a matinee. We were great gluttons for theatre. That was in the late 1940s and 1950s: There was a background of seeing commercial theatre whenever we could and so, although in a sense we were cut off in South Wales, there were the Arts Council tours that came around as well as the amateur theatre which was very strong. We used to go to London quite a lot on holidays. So although I was somebody brought up in South Wales, which would seem superficially not to have many opportunities to travel to the theatre, I did; and of course I took all the theatre-world magazines and in fact knew more about what was happening in the theatre in London in those days than I do now!

'Then I went into National Service and directed the odd amateur show in Aldershot and after that went up to university to Oxford although I didn't do anything when I was at Oxford. Indeed I was trying very hard not to become too involved with theatre because I thought it was too much of a distraction to my studies. I was supposed to be reading Law; nevertheless I did a lot of college drama but mainly acting. At the end of my time at Oxford I didn't go up to the Bar. We were rather hard up as my father had died, so I went to look for a job in London and worked in a large insurance society doing quasi-legal drafting work. But, although the company was very good and I enjoyed the social side of my work, it wasn't really for me; and growing inside me was something that had been there all those years and which I had deliberately pushed to one side because I suppose in a sense there was a family expectation that I continue with law. Theatre wasn't quite a serious thing even in those days. Nevertheless I felt more and more that it was really what I wanted to do.

'Then I started doing a lot of amateur work in London at the City Literary Institute which is where I met Clifford Williams, who, in those days, was directing a number of amateur companies as well as teaching. I confided in him that I was really dissatisfied and if the opportunity ever came I would chuck up my job and go into the theatre. In 1960 he came up with the news that he had been asked to direct a play for the Welsh Children's Theatre Company, which was an ad hoc company that was created every year, funded by the education authority in Wales. It toured around schools and they wanted a company production manager, so I put in for the job. Because they didn't have a stage manager I worked there in several capacities, giving up my safe job in insurance, although it was basically only a three- or four-month job and if at the end of it there was nothing — then that was the risk. But I thought, well if I don't take it now I shall regret it all my life. So I did and sort of worked my Equity ticket.

'We did an interesting and, from my point of view, an extremely educational tour for three or four months doing one- or two-night stands in schools. After that I came out and there was no work for me, so I came back to London and slept on a friend's floor for a while looking for work but nothing came up at all. Then through Clifford again I was informed that they wanted a stage manager on the staff of the Arts Theatre for a season — that was 1962 — so I applied for the job as an ASM and was interviewed by various people including

Maurice Daniels, now at the RSC, and one or two other people and they said — well, there is only an ASM job, are you prepared to take that? It paid about £10 a week in those days. So I went in on the basis that if it didn't work out I'd leave. I did the first production and in fact stayed on and did six productions that season. It was a smashing season because there were so many people in the company whom I've got to know over the years who are extremely well known in the profession now — it was a wonderful grounding to meet people who were also starting at different levels. I was lucky of course that they didn't find anybody — I'm not sure that anyone even applied — for the job as stage manager for the season and literally, because I was the oldest of the applicants, they said — well you had better be stage manager. Which was better because I had £12 a week instead of £10! We did some most interesting things such as the first production of David Rudkin's *Afore Night Come*.'

Finally he joined the Royal Shakespeare Theatre becoming first assistant stage manager and then deputy stage manager at the London end of the operation at the Aldwych Theatre, and making the move to Stratford in 1965. Eventually he became general stage manager, a combination of stage director and company manager.

'As the years went by, because it was very demanding in terms of time, you came in first thing in the morning and didn't go home until last thing at night. Long days — my children, who were born in Stratford, saw little of me. I took them to school in the morning and didn't see them until the following morning. I won't say I was dissatisfied with the job but I certainly wasn't happy. Then in the mid-seventies there were changes in the administration and I said I'd be interested in becoming something like a deputy production manager whose hours are limited so I could get the occasional evening off. It so happened that within a year or two of my first saying this it was decided to have a production manager for each theatre with a production controller over us who is our immediate boss, and so I got the opportunity to become the production manager for the main house here.

'This meant I dropped the company management side of the job and retained the stage director side of it, taking on administrative responsibilities for the stage crew, prop staff, stage electrics and sound staff; but I have also become the middleman, as it were, between the designers when they come in and our own workshop and outside contractors who make things for us.

'Each year I'm given a schedule of the coming season and told what is coming in. I also know then who the designers will be — probably chosen by the directors. At this stage the production controller is involved because it is he who allocates workshop space and the use of outside contractors, and has to make the balance between the demands of the main house, Swan and Other Place at Stratford and the Barbican in London.

'Once things are decided we hold our first production meeting attended by the controller, the design assistant, head of the construction workshop, paintshop and any outside contractors and of course the designer himself and then we have a preview of the model for the set.

'He shows it to us and talks it through and explains it and then we decide how best to carry out what he wants — we have to listen to him as obviously he will have his own prejudices and likes and dislikes. But from this discussion we all decide, in broad terms, how to put it together. We discuss the materials and look at the possibility of maybe experimenting if we are not sure how a thing is done — one can delegate quite a lot of that and the various departments take upon themselves certain things. But I usually find that it is up to me to look for materials and deal with certain contractors, maybe taking the designer out shopping for certain things. It's a question of being an in-between man, a middleman, as much as anything, and also of keeping a strict record. If I'm doing the purchasing and ordering there has to be a precise record kept of costing so that we know we are within our budget. Again it's a thing we talk through together. A set amount of money is given to each production. The lump sum for each year has to be divided four or five ways for however many the number of productions. Then you find that one production demands more than another, or vice versa, so that after you have balanced the different demands from the different departments we then have to discuss among ourselves and see what can be done about the costing of each play.

'We have a good idea of how much conventional materials will cost, but if there are particular materials that a designer wants to use we have to go to an outside contractor to make up certain curtains or drapes or special textured floor cloth — for instance, *Midsummer-Night's Dream* at the moment required a particular sort of fabric which the designer wanted to look exactly like his model. It was more difficult as we had to go around and look for different samples, chase them up and get them in time and then have them made up. You have to do a very quick estimate straight away for quantities and then discuss prices, explaining our requirements, such as making sure it's fireproof, and if it isn't fireproof how you arrange for fireproofing to be carried out. Next you have to warn the contractors we had in mind to do the making up of this floor covering that it has to be made up with a tremendous number of irregular folds and creases in a free form shape, after which the suppliers then have to be contacted. We have to keep a friendly relationship with all of them. You usually have to explain that you want things extremely quickly, and Bank Holidays always seem to come in the middle so you are always pushing!

'Then there is arranging transport. Most companies have arrangements with transport contractors and have a delivery date of four to five weeks — we have to say we want it NOW!

'Occasionally you need strange out-of-the-way things. You rely on the experience you have of the previous productions you have done. You know Joe Bloggs did something for you years ago which was a little way-out and seemed to be a technique which might be appropriate in this case — maybe not exactly the same but you know this chap is flexible so you go back to him. Consequently I have a small group of people scattered around the country who are specialists and whom I can call upon to do strange things at short notice. For instance over the last ten years through using people with these different skills I think we have come up with some excellent weapons, especially swords, which are very hard-wearing ones. I have somebody making blades for me out of steel which is extremely long lasting. It's not the normal sword-blade steel because that wouldn't stand up to the treatment it gets in the theatre. When you consider that we do a show for almost two years and imagine two bits of steel being battled against one another consistently over that period, well ordinary swords are bound to give out. So I have found one particular outside contractor who makes these swords which will stand up to that sort of treatment. We do give hard wear to almost everything that we put on stage. So we are on the look out all the time for new techniques.'

One of the hardest tasks he ever undertook was finding the right kind of crutches for Antony Sher in *Richard III* (a story told by Sher himself in his own book, *The Year of the King*). Nothing seemed to meet the different demands of designer and actor *and* stand up to all the wear. In the end he was told: 'Roger, it's your problem, whatever you do you have got to make these things work' — 'so I just staggered away and started looking from scratch again.'

He tried the rural industries organization, COSIRA, a factory which produces crutches commercially; then someone from COSIRA found a furniture-maker who had been an engineer. . . it went on and on. The furniture-maker designed the crutches in such a way that there should have been no question of stresses or strains building up 'but still they were unsatisfactory, still we were getting breakages.

'I think we'd got to Mark 12 eventually before we came up with one that was satisfactory, by which time the Stratford season had ended and the company was in Newcastle. We had four pairs of the Mark 12 and he only used the first — the other three were hung strategically around the stage in case they were needed. This is a good example of the sort of thing you can get involved in.'

What does he think are the principle talents needed for his job?

'First, a sense of humour. Next I think being able to get on with people; because it's such an independent place you can't go around telling people what to do all the time. You have to suggest what to do, gently planting ideas, and I think you certainly have to give credit where credit is due because people do come up with wonderful solutions. It is good to have a fair amount of general practical knowledge, and patience is very important to a certain extent. You also have to have a head for paperwork. It seems to me there is more and more paperwork which is inevitable in any sort of job I suppose, the longer you stay with it and the bigger the administration grows. So things like time sheets on Friday take up an awful lot of your time and you just have to be patient. But I think I'm very lucky being in an organization where people have worked together for such a long time with each other.

'Sometimes there are problems because occasionally you find you don't know that something is happening; but you mustn't get worried by it because it's usually because someone has taken a short cut and they are getting on with the job anyway.

'The one thing it isn't is a domineering job. It's a middleman — a sort of trouble-shooter!'

Gillian Diamond, head of casting at the National Theatre.

The Casting
Director's Tale

It is only in romantic musicals that the unknown girl or boy is picked up more or less off the street to become the star of a show. Of course understudies do get their big chance, but it is the business of starting out in the theatre which is so desperately difficult and, even then, the average actor or actress is going to spend a large proportion of his/her time out of work. So obviously one of the most crucial jobs in theatre is that of casting director to a large enterprise.

Gillian Diamond is head of casting at the National Theatre and also the Theatre's only female Associate. She is quite blunt about how she began.

'I started as a shorthand-typist and always had the most awful problems because I just couldn't spell. I kept going from job to job and when I was still very young I worked at Canterbury Rep when Clifford Williams was running the company. I was keen to go there as I'd always been a lover of theatre — I really was at the first night of *Look Back in Anger* and when I was a teenager I saw just about everything.

'Then I went to work for Clifford for about two or three weeks. Years later when I was still a struggling shorthand-typist — I just couldn't get a letter back from my own shorthand — he invited me to come and be his secretary as he had just joined the Royal Shakespeare Company. Because he didn't dictate, I had to write all the letters so it suddenly became something else. There wasn't a literary department or a casting department then, so next he sent me round the towns to see plays.

'That's how I came into the job. I was at Stratford for about six years, then I went to the Royal Court, and finally I ended up here. Casting here is an enormous job — there are three companies in three theatres as well as transfers and tours and the studio. One of the greatest problems is permutating people — now if he's playing so-and-so in this play, can he play such-and-such in that, and then what happens to her. . .?

'I don't think I'd be happy casting a hundred per cent of the time every day of the week because you can't come up with that many ideas, but now I'm part of management I've other things to do, which is a good thing.'

So how does she set about looking for people?

'At Stratford I would hold endless auditions because that was the way they wanted it done there. The only way I knew of finding people was by their writing in, or agent's phoning or going to see them in plays. Then I would call them in and give them an audition. I would see the first lot and then those I chose from them would go back and meet the directors and that's how the company was formed. I did that for a long time.

'At the Court it was completely different because most of the work was new. Any director can conceive his own Hamlet and that Hamlet is how he sees the part being played, but in a new piece of work you are actually bringing the written word to life and that is far more difficult because it has to be exact. I learned for example that if you are doing a northern play — and we seemed to do rather a lot at the Court — you had to have exactly the right character. I think the hardest example was *The Changing Room*, which was about a rugby team. The actors not only had to be the correct personalities for their particular characters but also the right shape for the position on the field that character played — so they had to be physically correct as well as everything else.

'So I suppose I learnt much more about finding the individual quality of each and every person as opposed to Stratford where people joined a company for a series of plays. An actor there had to be able to play five or six different roles in a season and understudy many more. At the Court you selected for that one part in that play and that was all. It was going from one end of the spectrum to the other.

'Here it's somewhere in the middle. Each play is cast separately. There are company people who go from play to play but not that many. Each play takes its own identity and I think that makes for a stronger company. Stratford still contracts for a season but here they all come attached to one play, or they have two parts in two plays or even, with a bit of luck, three parts in three plays, so everybody's on a different kind of contract.

'Peter Hall did not think the NT should necessarily be a training-ground for actors but it should be a place where every actor, at some point, could come and have a season or two and then depart — to go off to the world and then come back. We have a lot of that; people come back all the time and also our doors are open to new people. It is far better for an actor, when he leaves drama school, to do a season or two in Rep, the longer the better, and not stand swelling the chorus in a big theatre like this because he will not learn. You do learn something by watching but far more by doing.'

The stage has always been an overcrowded profession but now it is getting impossible, she feels. 'There are — quite simply — too many actors. It's getting worse and worse and the amount of correspond-ence we get every day is heartbreaking. Now, with all the cuts, the butter is spread even more thinly over so many more projects.

'By rights an actor should go from part to part in a different situation because each time he achieves something he gets that much more confident, so therefore stronger with each role — he's stretched every time. There's no way that can happen today. It's having one job a year now, which is not what an actor should be doing. The only way round it is for fewer people to come into the profession. There are hundreds of drama schools all training people to be actors.

'What has happened now is that there are so many TV series that anyone watching thinks: "Oh, I can do that — I think I'll be an actor." I was asked a strange question recently at one of our talks on careers. Someone said : "Can I take a course where I do technical and acting and then decide what I want to be?" I said no, you can't, absolutely not. If you want to act, you want to act. You have to actually climb up that stony road. There are no short cuts. It's probably because there is so much pulp put out on television which is not serious acting, it's just behaviourism.

'The part of this job which is so hard is to hunt your way through all those millions to find the one that is going to be magic, and what worries me is that all the time there are huge numbers saying "see me, see me, see me". Who don't you see? How do you make a choice? Are you rejecting *the* one? I don't know. I just wish there were fewer coming in. There was a time when I was at the RSC when I used to go to every drama school and then I'd follow the actor, knowing he was at Liverpool or Ipswich, say. You knew where they were and what they were doing — but not any more. It's so difficult for them even to get experience. Reps now want plays with one set and four actors. . . .

'You have an enormous responsibility for the up-and-coming generation and you like to feel on top of what you are doing, but I fear now the applications have got on top of me. I know that every actor leaving drama school writes to all the Reps. So there are all those to begin with and then everyone else is writing too. Young actors need their Equity card and there is no other way but to write. What else do you say to an actor? Write around.

'Then they need an agent. Some are good and do go to drama schools so there is a chance you can be picked up without a card and that an agent will find you if you have a bit of magic. An eighteen-year-old actor can still be seen in his last term at drama school and taken on by a top agent who pushes a theatre to take him and give him a card.

'My advice to those who can't get work? Put on your own show. There's nothing worse than sitting around waiting for the phone to ring. Put on your own show somewhere, in a pub, anywhere, it's all practice. Keep doing it, for the longer you don't act the more your confidence becomes eroded and the one thing you need is confidence to actually go on and blossom.

'You have to believe in yourself. It's not like anything else where you can offer qualifications — there are none for acting. You just have to get out there and act — it's terribly hard. Acting is far harder than most people think. They see it looking easy and believe anyone can do it. I think they should all have a very hard look at themselves. I don't think it's explained sufficiently to would-be actors. They do their end of term show and people say "Wonderful" and they think that's it.'

Does she still go out looking for talent?

'Absolutely — at least two or three times a week somewhere. There are three of us in my department; we're all out about three times a week so we see anything from nine productions upwards. That's only the tip of the iceberg. We see dress rehearsals and previews here and understudies when they go on. The turnover of work is fantastic. This is a huge building but you won't find a space in it where someone isn't working. It's an extremely exciting and lively place to work — every day is different. Now we are doing transfers, tours, studio shows, which is more casting. The strength of the company varies between about 125 and 150.

'People are now interested in casting as a career. You ask them why, and tell them it's very hard, and they say they just like the idea. How do you get into it? The best way is to see a lot of shows — and many of those wanting to come in work in agencies which is a good way to start, or television. In TV you can join a casting office or start in the bookings department which teaches you about contracts.

'The demands on a casting director are very hard, to actually create and produce ideas that are the right ones for the play and for the director directing it — how he conceives it and how it is written. They talk extensively with me first. For instance David Hare is going to do *King Lear* so we have talked about how he conceives him, otherwise I couldn't cast it. Then Tony Harrison is doing a project and he has talked superbly on what he wants and what kind of people he needs. When Tom Stoppard was adapting *On the Razzle* all I had was a literal translation, so I phoned him and said: "I don't think I can even show this to an actor". He came all the way down to London and sat and read the first two scenes to us so we could get the flavour of what he was doing so we could cast it. On that level it's magical, when you can start getting the feel of how they want the play to be. I suppose it's a bit like making a meal. Casting is getting together the ingredients, rehearsing is cooking them.

'To me every production is like giving birth because the directors now realize that 80 per cent of the success of their production will be to do with who is in it. I'm not talking about star names. I'm talking about the right people speaking the lines.

26

'I don't know what the qualities of a good casting director are. I always say I have nothing to offer anybody. I have no wisdom. I have no academic qualifications at all. What I have had is an instinct for certain things and it must have been a bit of luck this was tapped when I was young. It's an instinct that a university education might have taken away.

'It's just that, although I don't even know what "that" is. But if it hadn't been there I wouldn't have survived because the demands are so hard. Basically then it's just that — an immediate instinct.'

The coronation procession in *Richard III* (Stratford 1984) showing Bill Dudley's impressive set.

The Designer's Tale

Bill Dudley has won a number of awards, not least for his designs for the National Theatre's *Mystery Plays*. But he did not intend to become a theatre designer. He trained to be a painter. Then he began doing some scenery painting.

'I started painting scenery and I found that theatre in the sixties, both amateur and the professional theatre, knew what they were doing, which way they were going. There was a sense of common assurance which I felt was lacking in the fine art world. I submitted a portfolio of work to a hero of mine, abstract painter Frank Alvare. He looked at it and at the very back I had included a robot ticket collector that I had made as a theatre prop and he said that had more spirit than my paintings; and to have your hero, the person whose paintings you were obviously copying, say that was your best work was very upsetting. I went out blinking back the tears but it finally gave me the authority to actually go over to the theatre.

'At the time I was a bit snobbish — I thought it was a lesser art form as it was an applied art in a way, but it had a fascination for me although I had always seen myself, from about the age of four, as "the artist". So therefore I did a post-graduate course at the Slade School of Art. At the end of the course I wrote all the usual sort of letters and some directors from the Royal Court came and saw my end-of-term show; from that I got a terrific run of shows — *Hamlet* at Nottingham which came into London and then *The Duchess of Malfi* at the Royal Court. Since then I have worked pretty consistently. I had one difficult patch where I took on too much work and let the director down and it got a bit silly, so I thought I'll start back at the bottom of the ladder again which is what I did. I had already worked at the National and done opera abroad so it was like in snakes and ladders. It was a terribly hard way of growing up.'

So how do you set about designing a major production like the Antony Sher *Richard III* for the Royal Shakespeare Company?

'After the initial phone call to say we'd do it, Bill Alexander (the director) said let's meet in a pub and tell each other the three worst ideas of how to do the play, then we'll get them out of the way as a joke. The first choice of both of us for the worst thing we could think of was that as it was 1984 we should set it in Orwell's Britain. Playing around like that was a good idea as we hadn't worked together before and it broke down the barriers. I thought the Orwell idea was a great exercise because it is just the kind of self-indulgent notion that is all too often done these days.

'I don't like Shakespearian tragedies set in Fascist states with machine guns and so on, mostly because of the language. The law of weapons and steel fights it fundamentally — you lose all the personal valour of swordsmanship and hand-to-hand combat if you fight it out with Armalite rifles. That kind of updating of Shakespeare just doesn't work.

'So, once we'd got that over, and knowing the play like most people do from the Olivier film version, I looked into what was the received truth of the period. It was a season when the company were also doing *Henry V. Henry V* is very much about the climate, the physical journey to the battles, the camps in the rain. You are transported by the Chorus figure with descriptions of the weather, the time of day, the kind of country and the tramping on the march. With *Richard III* you are not. It's not about that final battle, it's to do with medieval politics.

'It's a play set really in Westminster. I thought how sophisticated, how machiavellian the piece was. We know Shakespeare read Machiavelli like most writers of his day and he used that as a source. It is a play about central power. So I went to St Edward the Confessor's Chapel in Westminster Abbey on a hunch really and there I saw the coronation chair, the very seat of sovereignty, containing the Stone of Scone; and the table tombs of Richard II, Edward III and their Queens and, at the entrance to the Chapel, the tomb of Henry V. There, in one room, you have this fusion of medieval power politics in a dynastic sense, alongside the coronation chair itself. I liked the theatrical nature of compressing them in one place and I began searching around for a piece of medieval architecture that would fit the Stratford stage and encapsulate that room.

'I wanted to design the set with table tombs because I could see that if I laid them out as I'd seen them in Westminster and also in the Beauchamp Chapel in Warwick (where the Earl of Warwick is buried), then on stage you would create divisions. You would have roadways, walkways, corridors betwen them and you could create an evil imagery of the corridors of power. You could imagine Richard and his henchmen loitering around and sense the medieval paranoia of the court favourites — who's in, who's out? Is the Duke of Buckingham in? No, he's out now.

'Then I found in a book of architecture a picture of Prince Arthur's Chantry at Worcester Cathedral built by the very Henry Tudor who killed Richard III. It was the tomb of his youngest son who died early. So I hopped on a train with a camera and when I got there I found it even better than I thought it was going to be, a perfect gem of the English perpendicular sytle. It was the last period before the Renaissance hit us, the end of the English medieval period. So I thought that as it was the end of the Wars of the Roses as well, you could see it as the final, sophisticated crown of the period.

'What was so nice was that it was miniaturized and it was so perfect I could not improve on the proportions. There was nothing gross in that chapel, so I did a photographic survey of it, a collage of photographs à la David Hockney into one impressive photograph. This gave me the general lines and then I did a tracing over that and photographically reduced my tracing down to a scale which would suit Stratford. The series of verticals creates extra depth and makes the stage feel deep and with the grill work you can show sinister shadows coming through the spooky corners. I hoped that you saw, with the table idea, a sense of all those people lying backwards, a sense of time and dynasty, and the immortality that Richard craved of founding his own line.

'To that end Bill developed the idea further and had the corpse of Henry VI, and all the other victims also, laid out on beds in stone-coloured robes, for they are the next in line for those stone tables. They were figures in the river of time. I would love to have had another twenty foot of depth to have had more kings going back but you had to draw the line somewhere!'

Sher's much acclaimed performance was aided by the fact that he looked like the 'bottled spider' described in the play's text. 'It was grotesque, wasn't it? The bottled spider. . . . The costume took a long time to evolve. I did a drawing showing that shape and Tony had also done some, before the production really started. I looked at them because he wanted to use crutches and he also wanted a club foot as well. But the whole thing about the spider image which is so frightening is the way it has speed but no weight, it's got an airless contact with the floor and if you give it a club foot you make it drag. So with the long tabard garment with its sleeves you have two extra legs, then you've got another two for the crutches, then you have his own two legs. We also talked him out of excessive facial make-up and then we had a special effect for the hump on the back.'

One of the high spots of the production was a marvellous corona-tion procession. 'It's after that it all goes downhill for him. He can't handle it once he's got it, he's bored with it all so it's going to be a short life and a merry one. This man is lost unless he has another country to conquer so what's he going to do now? There's nothing more to come.'

Quite different again were the *Mystery Plays*. 'They coincided with the opening of the Cottesloe Theatre and it was the first production to use its dance hall capability. It's great asset for us was that it had the ability to level off its floor flush from the stage right across to where the stalls' seats would be, and we were licensed to have 200 people standing down there and a further 200 seated in the higher levels.

'There is a Flemish miniature which shows a performance of a miracle play which depicts a saint being martyred — I think it is St Bridget — in the foreground, but behind is a building of wood that closely resembled the inside of the Cottesloe Theatre with people sitting at the upper levels, and right up among them is God's throne with a Jesus figure on it. Below there is a sort of stage manager figure, stage hands, actors and audience all mingling. The parallel was that we should take this medieval piece and slightly update the language — but keeping the rhythm and sense of the alliterative verse — then cloak the medieval idea with the things of this century. Maybe not the latest, up-to-the-minute things, but things that people over the last two or three generations loosely understand, things that are classics in their own right and haven't changed much in twenty-five years. Things that you take for granted.

'The parallel is that of the Catholic ceremony of breaking the bread and drinking the wine and saying this *is* Christ's blood because we say it is, this *is* Christ's flesh, which is central to the Christian ritual. For the *Mysteries*, therefore, we'll say this carpenter's donkey is a real donkey and we'll stick a straw head on one and sit an actor on it who says he's Christ and we'll carry it about and he will become Christ. So we found many modern-day equivalents to medieval things, common-place objects. We said to ourselves that in those days they would solve their problems by using ordinary materials from local suppliers. They would have to. Sailors and boatbuilders would rig ropes and blocks, pulleys and tackle to raise things. They had quite elaborate effects. So at the theatre we used a fork lift truck to put God in heaven. That was a direct equivalent to what they did.

'We took the shows to Edinburgh and did them in the open air. We couldn't do Noah's flood as we did in the theatre so we hired a builder's skip and put Mr and Mrs Noah into it. It looked like a boat and we popped a little wooden kennel inside with them and we put it on a lorry and got the driver to operate on cue, so that as the flood water rose he lifted up the skip with them in it. The actors shook long pieces of blue silk underneath for the water. Its very naïvety fitted with the plays' style. When you read the text the literal belief in the Bible gives you the same effect as looking at a naïve painting; it is both moving and can make you feel very grand and patronizing, but I'm not so sure about that kind of feeling any more. Science is coming round to thinking that perhaps the Bible is correct more times than we think but, apart from that, a naïve faith is moving because it has certainty.

'Then, at the end of the forty-eight plays, they would show the Last Judgement. We thought that would be in terms of a wheel, the wheel of fortune, so I wanted to find a circular image, rather like a Michelangelo painting with Jesus in the middle and God on top. In most of the plays we used the floor which was the human plane, as you might say, the surface of the earth. So in the Last Judgement I wanted to move into more God-like ideas, the realm of the spiritual. I wanted a vertical plane and cast around for what to do.

'Then I remembered Stanley Spencer's wartime pictures of the Glasgow shipyards with welders and riveters inside the stomachs of ships, humanity in a nightmare scene that I found intriguing. I'd also seen the National Theatre building when they were putting in the Olivier revolving stage. It's like a sunken gasometer. I remember seeing two men welding away, some thirty foot down. You know the strange light welding torches make which is also in Stanley Spencer? That is the light of doomsday — not the comfortable old Magicoal fire red; it's the white heat of the nuclear explosion, far hotter than cosy red coals and it would work, it would be jagged and shocking as if the whole thing was alive, rather like the metal mesh on top of the dodgems. So I combined the elements and had people in a cage going around a wheel of fortune against the light of welding torches. The world would be spinning and that and Armageddon was combined into one image. So that's how it came about and it happened to combine well with the bridge we used for the rest of the plays. I could disguise the wheel, which was there all the time, by making it look like a catwalk. Then I put the lines of latitude and longitude on to the wheel to clinch the image of the world and poor suffering humanity in the way a medieval cartoonist would represent it, with people out of scale and the world — rather like a political cartoon.'

Bill Dudley's work is very varied, from the table tombs of *Richard III* to exquisite costumes for Sheridan's *The Critic*. How does he like to work?

'Well, I don't lock myself away or anything. I start off usually by doing elaborate doodles before going on to more elaborate sketches. I work everywhere — especially on trains. I might draw the same thing several times trying to say what I'm hacking at; then I work it into a model, quite an elaborate and highly finished model eventually. I think stage design models are always a little silly, in some ways at least, in terms of the work we put into them, how accurately and lovingly we make them — not like TV models which are often just pasted-up drawings.

'We go to considerable pains to get them right because we're working for the naked eye, so we make the models look as close to what the actual set will look like as possible. There is a kind of cult of fine miniaturization of models which, however temporary their nature and however little time they are required for, is one of the pleasures of the job. Because it's only once you've got a really good working model that you've something real to take around the workshops so that people can properly understand what you want.'

Coming up, when I spoke to him, were designs for *A Midsummer-Night's Dream* at Stratford and plans for *The Tempest* at the National, so he was working flat out. He and the director were thinking of setting the *Dream* in Greece — as Shakespeare wrote it — although not necessarily classical Greece. 'I can see Theseus and his courtiers as the kind of men — those little circles of overweight men — who sit around in Greek cafés and talk and do as little as possible. The girls are all much younger than the men; Demetrius and Lysander are perhaps ten years older than Helena and Hermia.

'Hippolyta too. We're going to have different actors for Theseus and Oberon but the same actress for Hippolyta and Titania, for here she is three nights from the wedding and she's having second thoughts. Theseus is a kind of Onassis figure, the older man, and she has not met a younger man that attracted her so the play is about her dream too. Oberon is the younger man she might have married.

'Bill Alexander wants the fairies to be story-book children's fairies but also have some of the old idea that fairies are really still-born children.'

The Tempest too will hardly be conventional. 'As we are speaking I'm trying to get the revolve stage at the Olivier to work for the first time in ten years! It was designed to do too many tricks and I've proposed a method of simplifying what it does so it can be used on a regular basis for big shows.

'Bill Bryden sees Prospero as a kind of Fellini figure and we're setting it in a film studio. We're going to try and do the storm scene on film. It's quite a problem in the theatre as often you can't hear a word of it and it's just people bellowing in semi-darkness. But you can film it and project it on a screen. Then, as the ship is wrecked, the screen tears as if it was the mainsail of the ship and reveals behind it a deserted film studio with Prospero as the film director — the nearest equivalent to the worker of miracles. The whole story becomes a work of his imagining as he can conjure up anything he likes.

'So the characters are in his own mind — a film he might direct. And after he's conjured up this storm the revolve moves and sinks and does things and then out of the depths come these Elizabethan characters. . . . All the tricks of stage sounds and lights and wind machines and so on can be used quite literally, for it is like magic to them, you see. Did you ever see any of the great backstage movies and the fantastical places film studios or stages can be? The journey for the shipwrecked people takes them into this world and it becomes an island, an island of the mind. I do think it's a very strong idea and way of doing it — it's true responsive poetry.'

What is obviously crucial to a designer is his relationship with the director, and Bill Dudley works again and again with the same people. 'I have about three directors I like working with all the time on a rotating basis — Bill Alexander, Bill Bryden and Richard Eyre. That's the way I prefer it. You believe in their taste and that it is right — it's an act of faith. You know their styles and ideas will accord with your own. It's better like that — two or three friends you can work with on a show-to-show basis. That's how it works best for the designer.'

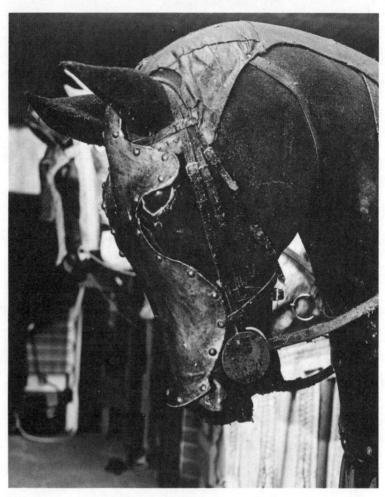

The RSC's horses wait patiently in the wings for their turn on stage.

The Property Maker's Tale

5 Bill Lockwood is head of one of the busiest and largest props departments, that of the Royal Shakespeare Theatre at Stratford.

He is a modest man. People in general, he thinks, are not interested in what goes on behind the scenes in the way they are fascinated by actors. 'The only time I've had a biography in a programme was when I was one of the co-designer's on *Poppy*. Farrah did the set, Alexander Reid did the costumes and I designed all the props and special effects, but normally in a programme, no, it's just usually the actors, the company.'

How did he get into the business?

'I followed a brilliant elder brother through school but I was sent down from the school I was at. My parents despaired. But I was very good with crafts and arts so I actually came here as a very junior junior for four years. Then I thought to myself, "well, this is ridiculous, I've got to go away and do something", so I then went to art school in Leamington and from there to London to study for my Diploma. After I got it I went to work at the Royal Opera House in Covent Garden for a short while and then the then production manager here, Desmond Hall, asked if I'd like to come back as the assistant head of props. I came back in 1964; Jerry, who was then head, retired in 1965 and I've been here in this job ever since — it's a long time.

'It's a big department. At the moment we employ ten and a junior and we try to make everything from dead cows to carrots! We are extremely busy. Obviously our main responsibility is to the main house here in Stratford but there is also The Other Place and the Swan. There are more occasional London openings and we are involved to some extent with new London productions, but there are all the transfers from here and we have to tart up what's required.

'We cover the whole spectrum. But materials and the ways we deal with them have changed tremendously and we are always finding some new way of doing something. Working with this company is good because we have tried to experiment with new skills or with the new products which come on to the market. Some of these are wonderful and we find we can adapt them to whatever job we are working on. We use materials you would never think of.'

Behind him on a stand is a disembodied head. 'That head of Alan Howard, for example, is made in isopon which is used in the motor trade for filling car panels when you've had a crash. It smooths out dents. Why use a car metal filler? Because we find we can work it better than anything else for that particular job, it's a very good medium to work in.

'Now, too, we are going into the polypropylenes and polyvinyls instead of the polystyrenes which were fairly new in the 1960s. Polystyrenes have been banned in some areas, including the GLC, because although they are fireproof they give off poisonous gas in a fire so that is why we have gone for other synthetics. We use polyurethane too. It comes in big blocks or you can mix your own; it's a two-part mix and it's very versatile. It was used for the big lions in *Othello*, for instance.

'We make and treat all the furniture used on stage. If the furniture is new or made of new wood then we "distress" it. We've actually gone as far on some occasions as putting woodworm into furniture, not because the audience can see the holes from where they sit but because it gives the furniture the right overall effect. In fact the more you distress wood the more aged it looks on the stage. You can never put a brand new piece on stage, it always looks wrong. So we set fire to it and then wire brush it and that brings out the grain. But that's the old way of doing it. Sometimes now we use a newer one. You can sand-blast it and that is done under special conditions. We don't have our own sand-blaster but there is a gentleman locally who will put his over a piece of timber; it takes away the softness between the grain and leaves it risen and that looks pretty good. Then, of course, you use different dyes and paints to stain it.'

Props had made an enormous tallboy for a recent production of *Les Liaisons Dangereuses*. 'That was made here. The designer gave us a rough idea of what he wanted just verbally. We had a book showing us a tallboy of the right period but of course it was a normal size, you could actually reach the top drawer. With the one he wanted you would need a step-ladder but we managed to make it to scale. Actually we cheated quite a lot on that eighteenth-century furniture for *Les Liaisons* by using plastic mouldings as opposed to real carvings or real mouldings, because there just wasn't time. It takes a lot of time to produce a genuine moulding. So quite often now we buy those little plastic carvings which you can find in any DIY shop and we dye them and treat them before we apply them, distress them a little, and you'd never know.

'We do now buy in a number of items. For instance you can find quite good cheap brass, copperware and tinware now, the kind of thing we use in stage goblets and plates, so we no longer have to make them. But furniture you almost always have to make because it just doesn't stand up to the wear and tear of changeovers and production. Today's new furniture wouldn't last a season so that's why we make almost all our own.'

So how does he set about a new production?

'The first thing is that the designer makes a model and presents it to the director and the director and the designer then talk through it and the director decides what changes he would like. Once the model has been accepted, it goes into construction and then you know that you are going to have to make a certain number of tables and chairs, or a lion or a statue or a cannon or a carriage, so those can be fed into our programme.

'It is not until the director is in rehearsal with his company that the individual props come out. An actor might feel it would help him to have a bag or a box or a book or a goblet and that list comes out and is brought to us during rehearsals. So we start off on the production by working on the main design statements, like the furniture required, the carriages, the beds and so on. Then we move to the smaller hand props.'

What control does the director have over these?

'Not a lot. Occasionally of course a designer may come in with a design for a specific item or even no design sometimes and you just have to try and interpret what it is he wants. When he then sees it actually in a three-dimensional form he perhaps would like a change here or there or he says it's not quite how he visualized it, so we adapt it for him.

'We don't normally tackle personal jewellery unless it's a particular item like the metal crown used in *Richard III*. We made that because it had to be brass and the jewellery girls down in the Wardrobe Department just did not have the facilities for working in metal so if it's a metal object then we do it. We also do all the orbs and sceptres for kings but the dividing line can be difficult. On some productions you do have a separate designer for the set props and a designer for the costume, and costume can involve things like canes, sticks and bags. A costume designer might get Wardrobe to make the bags and buy in the sticks — he wants to ensure they match in with his costumes — but usually we make them here along with the personal props for an actor. What we never touch is costume.'

One item Props usually has to deal with is bedding and drapes. For a recent production of *Othello*, says Bill Lockwood, 'we laid in what we thought was going to be necessary and started measuring up for the nuns' veiling for the drapes and so on and then the director told us what he had in mind — rubber sheets! Apparently only rubber sheets would give the sculptured effect on Desdemona's bed that he wanted. Have you ever tried to *buy* double-bed sheets in *rubber*? Well obviously no ordinary warehouse stocked them and medical suppliers don't go in for double rubber sheets, so in the end I was reduced to going around the sex shops in London and I might say they do give you the oddest looks even there. But that was difficult too — they kept offering them to me in red or black and said they didn't have them in white. The mind boggles at who buys red or black double-bed rubber sheets. . . . Eventually I found one who could supply me with them in white, but they were an awful problem because you can't clean them like cotton.

'But on the whole *Othello* was quite straightforward. The worst production I have ever worked on was the double bill of *Timon of Athens* and *Two Gentlemen of Verona* we did some years back because nobody knew what anybody wanted, it was delayed, and just about everything went wrong.

'The biggest single prop list we have ever had to tackle was that of *Nicholas Nickleby*. It was colossal and contained literally hundreds and hundreds of props.' (The RSC was just about to revive it which was something of a headache.) 'We do have certain props from last time from when it came back from the States, but after it had been filmed for television we decided they should go into general circulation. We have a vast storeroom where we store old props and obviously we use what we can because of costs and a lot of it has already disappeared, re-cycled into other productions. We managed to identify most of the furniture but again there are problems, for it is to be a touring season as opposed to the original production where so much was actually built into the theatre. The set was actually constructed in place in the theatre so to get rid of it we had to take it all to pieces. For this season we are doing eight weeks in one place, a season in another. We're then touring it before it goes back to the States so the property list will have to be reduced in size, but it's still colossal.'

So to individual specialist props. . . such as the 'horses' rode by Richard II and Bolingbroke in a production of *Richard II*. 'We made the originals out of cane but unfortunately we found they lost their shape very quickly and they were quite heavy because we had made them out of baskets and then draped them. So then we went into fibreglass and that was a very good idea because they lasted extremely well. We now have eight 'horses' and two 'ponies' in store and when we need them we just re-dress them. But the two horses we used in the last production of *Richard II* had to be much, much bigger, so these were specially made and we based them on Clydesdales, huge work horses.'

The actor Antony Sher, in his book *The Year of the King*, had a good deal to say about the difficulties he had had with finding the right crutches. A look of pain crossed Bill Lockwood's features as I asked him about the *Richard III* crutches. How many different types had he tried, I asked?

'Ninety-two. . . We produced *ninety-two crutches*! We tried everything from National Health elbow sticks to light-weight steel; then we went on to titanium which is used in space flights and from there to a special kind of light-weight steel used in Olympic racing backs which is very strong and very light. We even tried American hickory. What was wrong with them you might ask? Well, he went into rehearsal with NHS sticks and he liked the weight and got used to them and whatever we did he just kept on going back to those, but in his performance they kept on breaking all the time. At one point we had bought virtually the entire country's stock of elbow crutches so that all the poor little people with broken legs must have been hopping around waiting for Richard III to decide which sticks he wanted. In the end we achieved it by using the American hickory and bound it in wire to help prevent it from splintering.

'Nor was that all. Next came "the Hump".' (Sher in his book had referred to the hump as 'the money' because it cost so much.) 'We could have made it here but no, they wanted this particular guy to make it. He did all the make-up for *I Claudius* and he made Derek Jacobi's nose for *Cyrano de Bergerac*. As he charged £500 for the nose, and if you think how many noses can fit into a hump, it will give you some idea of what the hump cost. Mind you he has to buy in the materials, then there's the time involved, and obviously he's got to charge overheads and things whereas our departments are always here so it's always within the budget. When they finally got the thing they didn't like it. . . .

'Making everything in-house does keep the costs down. If you had to break down each show individually and we ran this department as a commercial concern and charged the show the money it costs to run the department then obviously their budgets would go up tre-mendously. That is why we usually make that kind of prop.

'We've made humps before. We did the Caliban hump in *The Tempest*. We made a cast of Bob Peck's back and then made a deformity on it on the plaster mould after we had cast it, and we found that we could get the right effect by using cauliflower florets as they had the right kind of texture — so we put those all over the clay. Then we cast it.

'From that we made a kind of rubber suit which was, of course, horribly hot and kept moving up and down. So in the end it was built on to a padded waistcoat which the wardrobe produced and then we covered it in the rubber, moulded around cauliflower florets, then went to Brenda in wigs and she blended the joins from the latex to his body.

'For an earlier Caliban, played by Barry Stanton, his whole body

41

down one side was deformed and so we actually cast the whole of his trunk and then made him a complete rubber top. Again it was very hot, so we had to make three because once worn it had to be cleaned, otherwise it would have been dreadful.'

What were the strangest requests he had had from individual actors? Well, it was not possible to name names but it seems that some actors who have to wear tights or other close-fitting costumes and don't feel nature had sufficiently endowed them will get Bill to knock up some kind of a codpiece. . . .

Obviously it is most enjoyable when Props people can give their own skills full rein. 'I designed all the props and furniture, for instance, for *Antony and Cleopatra* in the Romans season. I really did enjoy that. Chistopher Morley was in charge of design and I did all the props and furniture myself. We researched for several months the period from 400 BC to AD 300 and, being skilled in the business now, I knew exactly how far you could make bends in timber for the thrones and the bed which was actually based on that of Tutankhamun. It was a tremendous success at the end of the day, with the colour, the silks and the fans.

'*Poppy* too. Obviously as it was a semi-pantomime we had to have pantomime horses and it was such fun because we'd never had to do anything in Shakespeare or his contemporaries like that before, so it was a real challenge. The horses had to wink and blink and cry and blush and I don't think the two actors who played the horse, Randy, got sufficient credit. Chris Hurst was the front end and Andrew Thomas James the back and they were superb. They made him come alive they were so wonderful, and they didn't get the credit because people saw them simply as a horse. Everyone identified with that horse and when it died they couldn't believe it. Every time he was shot I cried. I did! Because he was so real, so human.

'We carved the heads in polystyrene and then cast them in thin fibreglass and then we lined them. We used something rather like the handlebars on a bicycle with "brakes". You pressed the right hand or the left hand to make him wink or blink and open his mouth and you pulled down to make his ears erect and then we had an enema syringe for making smoke come out of his ears. The female horse, Cherry, had to be able to cry as well so we incorporated the kind of pump used in motor cars for windscreen washers.

'What you do have to be is versatile. For a recent production of Brecht's *Happy End*, which toured with *The Taming of the Shrew*, we had to make fourteen "bodies". We based them on a maquette, which is the wooden jointed figure artists use, but we didn't use the shape in the round. We used it flat and then we made the shapes in plywood and hinged them together. Over that we used polyurethane foam for the body shape and over that again, stockinette, and then we dressed them. We cast one of the boy's hands for the hands on all the bodies. They looked tremendous, as when they were picked up or helped off they looked like real people who were unconscious or stumbling.

'Then for *The Shrew* we did the banners and the baskets — and the babies. Two of the chaps here actually wove the huge wicker bassinet in cane because we couldn't buy one that size. Then we "distressed" that as we distress furniture. You can rarely put even an individual new prop on stage; it just looks so wrong because under the lights it shows up every detail of it. We are always breaking stuff down. For instance, if you buy a pewter plate you can't put that pewter plate straight on stage because it would just blind everyone under the light; so we have to break it down until it looks authentic from the audience and the same goes for brass and copperware. It's quite difficult being down the road from the theatre because we have to do the breaking down in this building and you can go too far sometimes, and then when you get it on stage under the lighting of the production you find that you've gone too far and you have to bring it back again. The other problem is getting an actor out of rehearsal to work with him on a particular item. Once he's got it he wants to hang on to it of course and you can't prise him away from it.

'Even documents have to be specially treated. We make them look old by using a mixture of varnish and meths, used very weak so that it's almost like cold tea but of a kind of coffee constituency, then we tone it down.

'There's so much we make and have great problems producing that I don't think the audience even notice. Little things which can take a lot of fiddling, like this. . . .' He produces what appears to be a second human head. 'This was for Brian Blessed as Buckingham. He came down here and I did a full head cast, vaseline everywhere. For that you put them in a bathing cap to keep all the hair out of the way. Unfortunately Brian had a full beard which caused even more problems. So I had to cover the beard with butter muslin coated in petroleum jelly. You take the face section first. Some people use straws up the nostrils but I just leave holes in the plaster. Then we do the back, making it therefore in two halves. We used a flexible foam with a thin rubber latex skin for the head and we had a set of dentures made by our local dentist and put them in the mouth. Then it went down to Brenda in wigs to put on a beard and hair. It was Antony Sher's request that it was a soft head because he wanted to stick fingers up his nostrils and pull his mouth about, which is why we used that particular method.

'We do heads, limbs, fingers, even entrails. . . . We did a dummy on an operating dissecting table for the Edward Bond *Lear* and there were entrails inside the dummy. Jenny Agutter actually fainted during rehearsal the first time she saw the entrails coming out.

'What can be difficult is getting more up-to-date props. We had a production of *Troilus and Cressida* set in the Crimean period or a little later and we managed to get everything eventually — things like tick-a-tape machines, field telephones, items from that period, could be bought or borrowed. Far more difficult was the production of *Merry Wives of Windsor* which was set in 1959. Not only is it difficult because it has to be right — because everyone from my generation remembers what things looked like — but 1950s stuff has suddenly become collectable and it's now very difficult to find. A smaller problem was *Nicholas Nickleby* this time around. We had to find someone who could make genuine Victorian muffins because the actors start off going around the audience with them.

What, I asked him, was the single biggest nightmare he could remember? 'I think probably a production of *Merchant of Venice*. It was the casket scene. We had the usual lead, silver and gold caskets but this time the director and designer wanted them made lifesize. There would be a skeleton in the gold casket, a joker figure in the second and Portia, played by Judi Dench, in the lead one. The actor playing the Prince of Morocco was not a very tall man. The first time he opened up the gold casket and took the skeleton out, it wasn't off the floor it was sort of on its knees. So we were asked to shorten it. First we took out some vertebrae but it still wasn't short enough so we were asked to shorten it some more. I said I'm not going to be responsible for what happens after this — it finished up looking like some kind of a monkey.

'Next we gilded the casket with its final coat. We used a cast of a girl who used to work here for the figure on the top because it had to be a woman lying on it. Then we finally got it on stage, at which point the designer felt it looked too bright under the lights so it had to be taken across to the paint shop at the last minute and sprayed down in tone. It had only just been finished when the stage prop crew needed it so they went across and fetched it. They closed the lid. But it wasn't dry. . . .

'While it was in the wings waiting to go on stage it dried. You can guess what happened next. It stuck. So along comes the Prince to do his one big scene and he can't get the thing open. After he had wrestled with it for some time one of the stagehands had to come on with a crowbar and force the thing open. The actor was *furious*, he was in a blind rage because his whole big scene had been blown by the

44

stuck lid of the golden casket. So he finally throws back the lid and literally wrenches the skeleton out — and it totally disintegrates. It had been re-joined too often. We never did find all the bits and pieces of bones; they probably fell through the cracks on the stage and down into the cellar. . . .'

Details of each show are carefully filed away in the theatre's archives. The files tell Props exactly what was in each production and what it was made of and how. It lists the names and addresses of suppliers and the prices, although these latter, of course, have usually altered by the time they are referred to again. 'It's very good from every point of view to have something to which you can refer back, because you may have a design which is very similar to something you remember in the past and you can look it up and find you can get by with a slight alteration here or there and use it.'

Bill stresses he is only the head of a closely knit, hard-working team. 'My assistant, Peter, trained at the Central School of Art and got a degree. Glen our main carpenter is not a carpenter at all really, he's a professional cabinet-maker by trade and trained in Bristol. He is quite superb — his woodwork is excellent. He does all our wood-turning as well, as we have our own lathe. The others I have trained here myself after they had joined us as juniors. I would much rather train them here than have someone in from outside as obviously each studio has it's own way of working; people from outside will come in and perhaps their ideas are not quite the same as yours and you get a conflict of personalities.

'When a prop list comes in I like to be able to say "ah yes, that's for Glen, that's for so-and-so" and then I like the designer to talk to that particular person directly, the one who is actually making it, rather than to me and then have me transfer the designer's views at second or third hand.'

'Our job is to keep the actor happy. Some actors can be very difficult and we cope with them by being terribly sweet and nice and saying "yes it would work" and then trying to — well not exactly to con them — to encourage them to work it out a different way or to try out something else, particularly if they are unsure in a role. But obviously when they are on stage and they are unsure of anything then it can definitely affect their performance so we have to be very careful. Any prop on stage that has to break or collapse has to be foolproof because if it goes wrong during a performance it can throw the whole thing out.

'My aim is to be one hundred per cent reliable. But I'll say this. I hate crutches. And I loathe humps.'

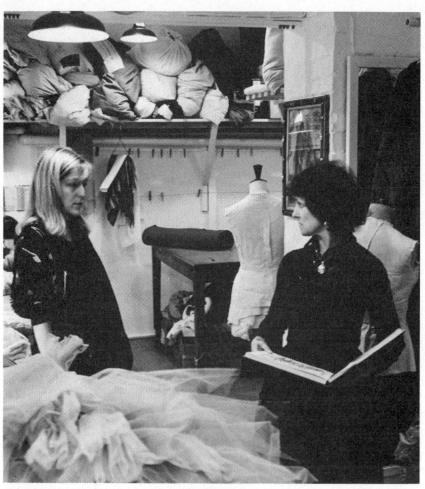

Norma Whittard (right), a cutter at the RSC, Stratford, in discussion with Claire Sherliker.

The Wardrobe Mistress's Tale

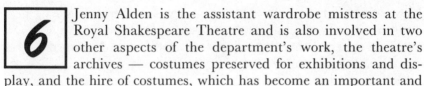 Jenny Alden is the assistant wardrobe mistress at the Royal Shakespeare Theatre and is also involved in two other aspects of the department's work, the theatre's archives — costumes preserved for exhibitions and display, and the hire of costumes, which has become an important and flourishing business.

She trained 'at an ordinary art college. I didn't do a special theatre design course because when I went there was really only one and that was at the Central. Nowadays we do have people who have done such a training or one of those costume courses which are specifically for wardrobe people. Also in those days you found a lot of designers who had trained at the Slade. They had started out on a Fine Art course and then digressed into theatre. They produced lovely sets and designs. Now we seem to get many designers who are more involved in just sets and how they are constructed and are not terribly interested in costume. Or you get in a situation such as we had on a recent *Othello* where one designer, Ralph Koltai, did the sets and another, Alex Reid, did the costumes.

'I first came to Stratford during the 1965–6 season. I came just as a sewer. I'd already been in touch with them saying was there any chance of a job. Then, in the middle of that summer, Reg Samuel, who ran the wardrobe, contracted me out of the blue and said he had been badly let down and would I like to come? So I just turned up in the middle of the season and I worked on three plays. It was the year Glenda Jackson was in *Love's Labour's Lost*.

'I stayed for eighteen months that time. The last show I did was *The Revenger's Tragedy* which was the change of regime when Trevor Nunn came in. Everybody seems to remember those costumes but they were made on something of a shoestring and were terribly fragile. They were made out of lining material with a kind of aluminium backing which is designed to keep heat in and cold out, a dual-purpose stuff, but it was extremely brittle. They kept coming apart and everyone had to go around with a tube of glue. We did have to make lots of remakes but it looked sophisticated and marvellous under the lights on stage. They were all silver and covered in imitation crushed-up pearls. That was what used to rip your hands and if someone brushed past you wearing nylons you ended up with them being serrated. But the costumes didn't last; we couldn't keep them in the archives because they just fell to pieces.'

After that she worked with the Prospect Theatre Company ('touring out in the sticks'), at the Edinburgh Festival, then returned to Stratford in 1972 for Trevor Nunn's Romans season. She worked both in the main house and at the then new studio theatre, The Other

Place. 'I worked there for about three years which was as long as I could stand it. We literally had no money then. We were doing shows for which the entire budget was £100 to £150. It has developed a good deal since then of course.'

She returned to the main theatre when the head of department, Frances Roe, had to divide her time between Stratford and London, needing an assistant at each end so she could move between the two 'knowing the reins were being held all the time'.

Stratford, she says, has a big wardrobe department 'but I was talking to a girl from Stratford, Ontario, and she actually has eighty people working under her, but that's partly because they put all the plays on at once and then the wardrobe people virtually disappear. We have been twenty-eight to thirty-two depending on fluctuating needs. If we need an odd sewer then we bring one in. We do everything here. We cut and make up, we dye, we do all the hats and jewellery. We make nearly every costume. The only things we don't make are armour — we have an armourer, Terry Watts, who does all that — and boots, which often go to one of the specialist London boot-makers. We haven't the space to do boots although I think our two boys could take it on because they are very good and inventive.'

Show budgets, she says, can be flexible in the main house. 'A director or designer can suddenly decide there is something they want and you can say well there's no money; you know you only have £4000 and that perhaps £400 of that will go over one production weekend in overtime and such. But if they want something desperately and feel it's a very important part of the play or is absolutely necessary for a particular character or actor, then you find they will probably get it! It may push the wardrobe over budget but it can probably be organized so that it comes off someone else's such as music. It's really robbing Peter to pay Paul.'

When the RSC's London end was the Aldwych Theatre, the Stratford wardrobe did all the work for London shows as well, but that regime has changed somewhat although 'they do keep coming down here to see what they can use. The Barbican is like a hole with no bottom — things just disappear down there and nobody has any idea where to find them. They only have a very small wardrobe department and use outside people. The problem with the Barbican is that they have very little storage space and store in corridors which isn't very good for costumes. You invariably find too that something is missing. Occasionally you find it months later. I remember searching desperately for Michael Gambon's King Lear crown for exhibition purposes and they all kept saying it had been put in a skip, but it wasn't there. Then one day I was going through a property basket in the store up the hill full of bits of costumes and so on and I found both the Lear crown and the Julius Caesar laurel wreath nobody had seen for months. . . .

'When a costume designer brings in the designs they are photostatted. Then we talk to him or her so we know just what they want. It's easier if you can take your designer with you when you go to fabric or leather stores to buy because you can be quite sure what they want. If it's something that's fairly rare and they decide to go ahead with it, you should buy it then; otherwise you can go back for another two rolls only to find it's all gone and there's no chance of getting any more in time. Also you can make sure that the colours are exactly right or that fabrics can be dyed to exactly the right shade.

'The wardrobe workers then see the photostats and samples of fabric and know exactly where each kind of fabric is going to be used, and they then have a good idea of what that designer is aiming for with that particular costume — the volume of a skirt, the shape of a coat, for instance. If we are working on something that we are not too sure about from the point of view of the designer's effect, then we make a *taille* in calico or thin cotton and show them the shaping to ensure that the shape is right. Then we use that pattern from which to cut the costume. You can't take a risk of making a mistake with very expensive fabric or with suede or leather.

'Once that has been sorted out then the next stage is fitting, because you don't go too far with a costume before you have a first fitting; so that too much work hasn't been put into that particular costume until the actor is in rehearsal and knows what he is expected to do in the part. Also the director, designer and actor will have got together and seen the design and if there are any changes we won't have gone too far to incorporate them. Sometimes, by the middle of the rehearsal period, the way that character behaves can have changed quite a lot and you realize that what you originally set out to do might not be entirely right and you have to amend it. A costume can have four or five fittings depending on how complicated it is and also how involved the actor is with that costume. Sometimes we make up items specially for rehearsal out of cheap cloth, cloaks, skirts, drapes. If it's something they use and feel they need then you make a rehearsal costume piece for them in something that doesn't matter too much.

'Time is always the problem. I'm not in on the early production meetings. It depends a lot, of course, on the individual designer. Some, like Farrah, put the set up in the paintshop next door to us. So we all go and see it and he tells us what he's going to do and what the whole production will look like so that you are more personally involved in the making of the costumes. But so often here we don't get the designs early enough or we haven't been told which actors are going to play which roles. We say we need eight weeks, we rarely get even six but if we had, say, ten, we could organize it better and you could take on so much more.

'On the whole the Royal Shakespeare Company is able to buy the material of its choice for costumes, but leather — and many designers do seem to have a penchant for leather — is now often simulated. 'At the moment though we are having problems even with that. You have to use a kind of suedette, a fabric with a particular kind of pile on it, and the firm that used to make it departed back to France so we are looking around for English makers. We finally think we've tracked one down in the west country. Once it reaches here then our dyers can simulate it and treat it until it actually looks like real, worn leather. When you do this it means having to pay quite heavy labour costs because two techniques are needed to achieve the right effect — but leather is now tremendously expensive.

'On the other hand a real leather costume will last you for a very long time if you clean it and repair it well. It just goes on and on.

'But then you should make everything well. We had a student in recently from a college doing work experience and she kept saying to me: "I can't believe things are so well made, I can't get over all the leather jackets." She had two days in our hire department so she saw a lot of old costumes too. I said to her that stage costumes actually get much harder wear than your own clothes. They are on and then off, there are quick changes when they are dumped on the floor, they are picked up, shoved into skips, hung on rails in dirty corridors, carted around the country, cleaned far more than your own clothes are and worn almost continuously. At the beginning of the season when we don't have many plays in repertoire they can be worn for three continuous days from ten in the morning until eleven at night. Every fastener has to be foolproof.

'Sometimes you find you've made something and then you go to the technical rehearsal and realize there is going to be a quick change; either the designer hadn't realized that it was so quick or it had happened because he decided to change the costume in a different place from the one they originally thought of. You suddenly find you have to adapt the whole costume to get around it. It's partly a matter of practice.

'Sometimes designers do seem to want very difficult materials. They come up with stuff which isn't actually fabric at all and you find you're working in plastic or leatherette and materials which just do not want to mould to a body but should be used in a flat manner. So you use them and then they crack. We did a *Richard II* with lots of lords wearing costumes made out of a kind of leather cloth, and some of those were embossed too which made it even thicker. Then on top of that again we had to use a kind of fake braid, the sort of thing jewellers line their windows with, and they were very stiff costumes indeed. They didn't mould to the body, the actors could hardly move in them. We coped with it but not happily. You worry when you know something is just not suitable.'

On the other hand there are the costumes remembered with pleasure like the two marvellous draped copes for an earlier production of *Richard II*. 'There were two. One was in the very finest yellow and cream silk and there was yards and yards of it. Unfortunately that's just worn out. It frayed. The one we have on exhibition in the gallery is the other, the gold one with tiny accordion pleats. That was fraying around the collar and has had to be repaired but it does give you some idea just how beautiful it looked on stage.'

She has some drawings for a production of *Romeo and Juliet*. 'Now these show you just what is wanted. Nadia Bayliss did these. They are not at all conventional for the play — they are more modern, but they are fine to work from. The ladies wore dresses of knitted rayon and silk and the boys wore real leather and suedes and it all had to be piped. Some of the fabrics for the women were hand-knitted.

'Recently we had the 1959 *Merry Wives of Windsor* and that was a real turn up for the book. We worked from actual magazines for the period. We should have got the designs in December but they didn't come in until February when we were already working on *As You Like It* as well and for that we needed a lot of tail-suits. So we just went to Moss Bros and got the tail-suits from them. It wasn't worth trying to make them but we had to comb the fabric shops for *Merry Wives* to find the right kind of material designs. We had the Teddy Boy suit made up in Birmingham where there's a special and wonderful Teddy Boy shop which is absolutely authentic. We got everything there for that particular outfit — waistcoat, trousers, tie, shirt, coat and the shoes with the huge crepe soles. For the rest we had to make the trousers and pullovers because they were very different in the 1950s to how they are now. We had a bad time with the macs. They were very difficult to find. In the end we had to buy them from John Lewis and adapt them. We had to print some of the materials here too before we made them up. An awful lot did come from newspapers and magazines, such as the barmaid neckline on one of the dresses, and the pictures showed us too just how those large floral prints looked when they were made up. On top of that a lot of people actually remembered wearing those kind of clothes and they kept saying to us "it wasn't like that. . . ."

'The children in the play scene had to be dressed as characters out of the period which meant us going back to 1950s children's books to see what they should look like. Do you remember Noddy? We had to find out what Noddy and Big Ears actually wore. We also had a headless man and a skeleton. The children were a little bit embarrassed at first when they saw the costumes but later they loved them. I'm particularly pleased with the headless man. He's got a "head" which looks like padded shoulders so he sees out of his chest. On the day they did a special performance for the Ethiopian Famine they loved getting out among the audience with the collecting boxes. At the end of the play they were all on stage. As you know, with children, you have to have two casts but we put them all on the stage together. Two of the boys were dressed up as 1950s fairies. They wore rubber swimming caps with flowers on and frilly skirts and they weren't worried at all — they rushed to get out there at the back and shake their boxes.'

Hiring costumes is now a considerable business. 'An enormous number of people use our hiring department. They don't just want costumes for the shows we've done but costumes for all kinds of other plays too. There's been a run on *Amadeus* so we have many requests for eighteenth-century costumes. We've found we're short of women's costumes so we are going to make some. Then the next time it might be Edwardian and we find we are rather short of one kind of men's outfit and make those up. When we aren't actually busy on a show then we might as well work on the hire side, repairing and adapting and making up from new. It's all work experience for the wardrobe girls and they rather enjoy it. We hire to other companies, to lots of amateur groups, even to individuals.

'My other responsibility is for archives and exhibitions. If I really want a specific costume for that then I try and ensure it never goes near the hire department. In fact I'm known for removing items from the hire department to put away for the archive! The hire department would have everything if they could. If you have a photograph of an actor wearing the whole costume it's nice to have everything to go on exhibition with it. Once it's been used for hire it's no good for the archive because it's been cleaned so often you've lost a lot of what it looked like. For the archives it must be as close to how it originally looked as possible.

'It's very important to keep costumes in the archive both as part of the RSC's history and so that students and designers can come and see them. Exhibitions are of increasing importance too. We have our own costume exhibition in our own Gallery but our costumes also tour worldwide. We recently had costumes on show in Japan, then they went to Belgium, then the British Council wanted them for something else.

'I don't think you can ever say one particular show was the most difficult or was the biggest challenge. Each one has its problems — you're up against time or you can't get the right fabrics. The Romans season was pretty heavy going but you just take each show as it comes. It's rather like when I go and ask the stage crew what problems they have had on a particular set and they say well, nothing much — it's now all routine because the problems they had in the early days have all disappeared into the past once the show is into its run. They've been coped with. That's what you feel, too. You've coped with it and then you think, oh well, we did it and now it's on to the next one.'

Brenda Leedham, head of make-up and wigs at Stratford, making up Richard Moore.

The Make-up Artist's Tale

7 Brenda Leedham is head of make-up and wigs at the Royal Shakespeare Theatre at Stratford-upon-Avon. The department is always the scene of feverish activity and she speaks to you while continuing to work. Work in the morning is often cleaning and re-styling wigs for the next performance. It is very hard work and it requires very special people to do it.

'I get a lot of letters from people who really don't understand what a job like this entails. They say they want to become a make-up artist or a make-up designer preferably and can they come here to learn. Those specific jobs just don't exist. The people who decide what the actor is going to look like are the director, the actor and the designer and then, after all that, comes me, pretty near the end of the process. That's when they come to me and say: "This is the effect we want, how can you achieve it?"

'How difficult this is, of course, depends upon the show. If it's a show like *Richard III* then I have to say to the actor (in the last case it was Antony Sher): "Yes, I can make you look like that but there are definite drawbacks." Sometimes they don't believe me and go off and say they'll get a second opinion after which they come back and say, all right, do something else. . . .

'Sher's Richard was extremely difficult. He wanted a totally realistic crooked back from the head down the neck, right down the backbone, then down the arms. There was a scene where his robe would slip off and you would see him just from the back view and it had to look a hundred per cent real. Now that would be totally possible in a film or on television but it wouldn't be possible in the theatre — at least not in that particular show — because immediately before the scene where he showed his back, Shakespeare has written a scene where Richard III in total contrast is seen as rather a pleasant fellow, playing with the young princes. He had already said he wanted it coming over to the audience what a nice guy he was so the children would literally be climbing all over him. Whatever prosthetic was used for his back, there was just no time between the scene with the children and the coronation scene where the back was exposed to start sticking everything down to make it look real. We just had to say "this is quite impossible".

'So he agreed to end up with a more limited area being shown. Even that was difficult, although it was done with the very best quality soft and supple rubber, but really it was more of a props job than a make-up one. Fortunately we don't get such difficult problems all the time although even straightforward make-up, or what is apparently straightforward, can have its difficulties.

'Now take the current Othello. Ben Kingsley was more than happy

55

to achieve an effect on his own — with a little help from God. He went off and had a holiday in Morocco and thought that would tan him nicely. It was fine in theory except that when he got back he didn't have the back-up of a fine English summer; as soon as he went into rehearsal even time on the sun bed stopped dead because he didn't have a minute to get there. At one point they suggested putting a sun bed in his own home but he said there wouldn't be any point because he never had any time.

'So we resorted to overnight tanning cream, which he dutifully laid on, and it was quite a nice effect; but the moment he stepped on stage the director said "absolutely wonderful, but could it be darker?" There's a limit to how far you can go with overnight tanning cream. To compound matters the whole costume and indeed the set was being designed on the understanding that he would go a natural tan colour, which would not come off on the costume. Certainly all his headgear was white because they thought there'd be nothing to rub off from his face. On top of that the bed had had to have white rubber sheets for the scenes with Desdemona and any ordinary make-up would come off on them. So I had to try a complete body dye.

'First we tried potassium permanganate which we've used before. Ben had never used it but he was somewhat happier when we explained it was exactly the same ingredient as that in the overnight tanning cream. It wouldn't do something unknown to his skin. So we did that and we got his skin to quite a pleasant tone with a deeper colour.

'Next time the director saw him on stage he said he wanted it sootier so would I put a blackish wash with it? I achieved this by using eyelash dye, which is pretty innocuous as it's a vegetable dye. But it still comes as rather a shock to your average actor when he finds it has to be plastered all over his face. . . . Obviously you don't know how quickly it's going to take and you have to watch it very carefully.

'Now the show is running we see he carries on with the overnight tan and then puts on those two layers of make-up to achieve the right colour before the show. But this can still leave a problem, so we have tried investing in some all-bronze tablets. It may be a better solution than overnight tanning because, although the overnight tanning cream sits on the base of the skin and won't come off on his costume, the eyelash dye does and that's giving problems: believe it or not, some of the costumes are made from material which can't be cleaned, they can't be washed and they are terribly expensive. Apparently they wanted a look only those particular materials can give.

'I've gone into this at some length because it shows the measure of sophistication which goes into the job nowadays. Ten or fifteen years ago the director would say "I want a tan", or "black him up", and I'd just go out and buy pancake make-up and the relative sticks of this and that and lash them on. You knew it would stain the costumes but of course, in those days, they could be washed and come up clean.

'Then there's hair. If a person is racially different and has different coloured skin he will have a different kind of hair as well, and in Ben's case we needed more hair than he has got himself because he's thinning on top. I didn't design his wig. He came to me with a very clear picture of what he wanted, something romantic and Arabic. There are several ways of approaching it. Sometimes it is the director who will know exactly what he wants every actor to look like. John Napier, for instance, has every wart and wrinkle thought out. He will then set about convincing the actor that he wants him to look like that and have a wig like that. I'll then produce the wig and the make-up. Then you'll get the vague kind of director who says "something a bit like his own hair only longer" or the one who murmurs "give him something period" if you are doing a period piece, or simply "one to make him look older" or "younger". In those latter cases you have a free hand.

'But in this particular production of *Othello* we had an amazing succession of actors, starting with Ben himself, who knew to every hair what they wanted to look like right from Day One. From what they wanted we had to put the whole look together. Ben brought me photographs of how he wanted his wig to look: it had taken quite a lot of imagination as what he brought me were pictures of belly dancing *girls* — he knew that we were looking at girls' hair but that's how he wanted it to be. We discussed the colours and the streaks of light that would be needed in it and how it would be dressed and we had a lot of fittings without the designer, just Ben and me; then we took him on stage in it and the designer could go on from there.

'Stratford makes all its own wigs. Not least because some of the past experiences have been far from happy. The memory still remains of the wigs for a production of *Troilus and Cressida* ordered from a famous wig house. The Greeks were supposed to be all dark and the Trojans fair and the wigs were late arriving. When they did the Greek wigs were fair and the Trojans dark. . . .

'We buy all the hair from hair merchants — there are only two or three in the country who specialize in different qualities of hair. Where do they get it from? Well some does come from nuns and possibly it doesn't do to go into where some of the rest comes from — let's assume that most European hair comes from nuns. We buy it by the pound and we mix up the colours that we want or dye it to a colour we want, especially if it has to exactly match the actor's own hair. There is no point in just sending a sample in an envelope and saying "let me have half a pound of hair like this" because there is a very slim chance that they would get it exactly right. If we mix it up on the spot while we have an actor or an actress in, we can look at the whole range of hair colours with the person actually present while we sort through it. The marvellous thing about making everything within the department is that we are all involved. The actors come in and say "how's my wig coming on" and they see all the work that goes into it; and it's very good for them because they'll take more care of it when they receive it while we can keep a constant check on it all the time.

'We do use hair again, it's wonderful stuff. I've got hair here in wigs stored away that are thirty, forty, fifty years old and belonged to Sir Ralph Richardson, Vivien Leigh and people like that. Hair lasts so well, although it depends on how it is treated. A little piece like this (she shows me a small fall of curls) will be put in rollers and then into the oven for an hour, then combed out and made curly. Then it's made into a bun and then put right up on top. It has to be used again for the evening performance so the whole process has to be gone through again. All the things happen to it that happen to your own hair. It gets dull and lifeless and splits at the ends and dries out and has to be carefully reconditioned. If a wig has to have a great deal done to it for each performance then we try and make a duplicate so that the hair gets a rest. If it is just a straightforward female wig with a long fall of natural hair, it's naturally easier to keep it in condition. It won't need so much work.

'We work a very long day as we have to be here right through every performance. We try to work in shifts so that, as there are six of us, two are on for each play and we service the main house, The Other Place and the Swan. It is hard and it requires determination. Nowadays the basic training is the City and Guilds Hairdressing Course. Then we also like them to have A levels in English and Art. When we take on a new entrant they spend two years in this department learning about stage make-up and stage hairdressing, all aspects of which are rather different from what they would learn at college.

'We are the Hairdressing, Wigs and Make-Up Department. If it's not costumes or props, then it's us. We do all of it. If you were a make-up artist and I gave you an eighteen-year-old actress and told you she was meant to look a hundred, then you would go away and make her false-teeth, a false nose and a bald head and then a wig; you would fit all those things on to her and arrange the pieces of hair which went on the wig which fitted over the bald head. You would dress what there was of the hair, you would stick all the false pieces on her and then make her up with the necessary make-up. You cannot do one thing, just hair and wigs, without the other, make-up.

'There was a time some years ago when we did try and split it and we had a hairdressing department and make-up department but it didn't work. You found yourselves fighting over things like who fixes the false eyelashes and who gets to put the hairs in a wart! That's really rather stupid. So you see it is just not possible to split it up.

'A make-up artist wants to be responsible for the whole thing. That's the fun of the job, to aim to produce a complete appearance. You find yourself become quite a specialist in the oddest things. There was a time when the directors here seem to be heavily into syphilitic sores and other nasty diseases which showed up on the skin. I had to pour over medical books full of foul-coloured pictures and I also got advice from consultants in the medical profession. I think there are still boxes of sores lying around somewhere. . . .

'You've got to be able to take the responsibility for an actor and to be able to work fast. You have to be able to do everything you want to do in the limited time you are allowed — you only get your actor half an hour before a show.'

What, apart from Richard III's crooked back, had been particularly difficult?

'I think the single most difficult thing I've ever tackled wasn't actually for here. We help out other companies in other places when they have particular problems in our field, and the Belgrade Theatre in Coventry did a Christmas pantomime for which they wanted a giant with two heads, a happy one and a sad one. It was the sheer size of the job that was daunting, but it was a terrific experience. They used two very tall actors in the same costume, both wearing lifts to give them even more height. I took a cast of each of their heads and then built up a mould from that to make their own heads appear much bigger; then I made the wigs for them. The two men walked around in the costume each with one hand behind his back and the legs hidden. It was a marvellous idea and it actually worked brilliantly.

'The other one I found particularly difficult was a character in a play called *Sons of Light*. Charlotte Cornwell had to play a girl who was encephalitic, which meant she had a large head and a big forehead. The tricky thing was to make her a head which could be got on and off in a second, because the play was put on in The Other Place where there is very little space and hardly any time for changing, although there was a huge cast and most people played several parts. Again that meant taking a cast of her head and then building up the new shape and making that in plastic, padding it out with foam so that it was very light and easy to cope with even with a wig on top. We had problems at first as to where to make the join of the wig to her face, but eventually we decided to join it under her eyebrows and then we let her hair fall down at the sides. But it was really tricky making it so that it would go on and off, yet fit like a glove.

'Your first responsibility is to the actors. You must do everything you possibly can to make them feel secure and happy when they go on stage, to make sure that whatever they might be worrying about then it is not either their wig or their make-up.

'Next comes the audience and they are far, far more sophisticated than they ever used to be. If you look at yourself in a mirror you don't wonder why you have lines around your eyes or, when you look at yourself in artificial light, consider you look washed out; you just see yourself in normal skin colour and that's how people expect to see actors. They are concerned if they sit there and wonder why someone has red blobs on his face, why someone else has obvious black lines around the eyes. They are really put off by a "stagey" appearance in actors.

'Technically one of the biggest breakthroughs has come from the fine lace on which wigs are now woven — it can be as little as five or seven denier in television, but even on the stage it is now so fine you need little or no make-up to hide the join. Right up until the early 1960s and 1970s in some provincial theatres, the fronts of the wigs were still make of cotton and whatever you did you could see the join even if make-up was plastered on. Audiences just don't want to see it — they are used to television. It's what they've been brought up on and they feel embarrassed now for actors if they can see joins in the wigs or obviously false bits and pieces. That's especially true of British audiences — it may be different in America — but a British audience embarrasses terribly easily.

'You just go along to a preview and listen and if anything goes wrong they really feel for those actors. They are right up there with them. That has really been one of the major reasons why heavy make-up has gone out. The actors, designers and directors would rather not be embarrassed by a heavy make-up and they would rather have none at all than one which was badly done.

'An elaborate make-up will only work if you have an individual make-up artist for every single person in a show, which is financially impracticable. If you just leave it to the actors then you are going to have a bad make-up in those circumstances because nobody can see the back of themselves or reach the parts other things can't reach. . . you need help, so it needs to be kept simple. It's been a financial restraint, it's been an emotional one, but it has made for much stronger theatre because you've taken away the barrier between the actor and his audience and what the audience sees is one hundred per cent real. So there they are, they look as believable as they do in television and in films, but much more so — there is that wonderful extra dimension because what is there is a living, human being.'

Stephen Ashby (left), an Olivier dresser, with Bill Nighy, who played Edgar in the National Theatre's production of *King Lear* (1987).

The Dresser's Tale

8 Sybil Coop had officially 'retired' from being a dresser at the National Theatre some years before I met her but, in fact, she was working as hard as ever as a dresser in a production of *Blithe Spirit* at the Vaudeville Theatre.

'It takes', she says, 'a good deal of intelligence to be a dresser and I mean real intelligence — not GCEs. . . .'

'I've always been connected with the theatre. I come from a family of musicians and my daughter is a pianist. When I was young I acted and I had a voice so I went into opera. I was at Sadlers Wells for twenty-eight years. I played all the page-boy parts like Cherubino and I also did Gretel in Humperdinck's *Hänsel and Gretel*. It was lovely.

'What took me into dressing? Money, I suppose. My husband died you see. He'd been a *répétiteur* at Covent Garden. But I was born into the theatre and I still think it's wonderful. It's funny — when I was in the opera I often used to think that I knew just what a dresser should be like, what they should do. I think that was a help.

'I was at the National Theatre for fifteen years, first at the Old Vic and then on the South Bank, dressing principals. Each principal has his or her own particular dresser.

'I leave nothing to chance. Everyone, of course, has to be there on the "half", half an hour before the show. But I'm there at least half an hour before that to make sure everything is exactly in its place. Pieces of costume which have been away to be cleaned or washed have to be checked out, whole costumes gone over if there is a double set. Each piece has to be laid out in exactly the order in which it will be put on while every item for a quick change is checked and double-checked.'

Her job begins before the play opens. 'Let's say it's something like *Hamlet*. The last *Hamlet* I did I dressed Laertes. The stage manager or head of Wardrobe would give me a notebook and pencil and I'd make a list of every cue and every item right the way through the show. I'd sit through the technical and the dress rehearsals, of course, no matter how long they take or how tired you get. You have to be prepared to be there all night if necessary but you get carried along because it's all so interesting.

'You have to take careful note of the items you know might cause problems — for instance, a certain type of sandal strap must always be in the right place, or then you have very complicated costumes with lots of chains and bits and pieces and so on which all have to be fastened the right way, sometimes very quickly.

'You can leave nothing to chance with a quick change. You have to stand in the wings in the dark and do the best you can — sometimes they have literally only seconds. I dressed Simon Callow in *Amadeus* and he'd a terrible quick change. He'd to get his shoes off — they just went up in the air anywhere — and then I'd go get a waistcoat and coat on together with no time to even see if they looked all right. But he's a marvellous artist, you know. Right out of the top drawer.

'It's particularly on those quick changes that you try and avoid what we call "panic stations". You have to be up and down and back and forwards like quicksilver.'

How about the actors? Has she had any trouble with any of them? 'Not really. If they start getting in a state I just get very stern with them and say "do this!" and "stop that!" and strip them off and get on with it.'

But however carefully you check everything out, however thoughtful you are accidents will happen. 'One of the early shows I did I had to dress someone who had a very quick change from a courtier to a bandit. I carried the costume up to the wings and as I arrived I realized I'd dropped half of his moustache. In those days I used to make up my eyes — what vanity! — and so I had to get out my eye-liner and draw it on his face.'

But there has been worse. Like the young actor who had to put armour on the leading man while he made a stirring speech. 'He got it right at the dress rehearsal but on the first night he put it on back to front and as costumes are always higher at the back it almost entirely covered up his face. You should have *heard* what he said when he came off. . . .'

Then there was the opening production at the new National, Marlowe's *Tamburlaine*. It came to the famous scene where the four kings who have been conquered by Tamburlaine have to pull him on in his chariot to his cries of 'Holla ye pampered jades of Asia!' and much cracking of a huge whip. 'Well they pulled him on and then the whole thing just stuck. Their costumes had got caught up in the wheels. Albert Finney, who was playing Tamburlaine, didn't realize it at first so he kept on shouting and cracking his whip and the kings strained and strained and nothing happened at all. I think in the end they had to get a kind of hoist thing and lift it off.'

'Then there was the Bear in *Hiawatha*. He only had seconds between going off in his Indian costume and then coming on again as the bear and there was an enormous zip down the back of his costume. On one particular night the zip stuck. I wrestled with it and wrestled with it and his cue came nearer and nearer; in the end he had to go on and I said "for God's sake don't turn round", which was hard for him as he was supposed to dance around and he had to try and do it facing front all the time.

'Zips are a nightmare. No matter how many times you check them beforehand they can stick, a tiny piece of material can get in, even a hair and there you are, they won't work. All of us so much prefer the old-fashioned hooks and eyes and you keep telling them but the designers won't listen. They use Velcro now for some quick changes, but the particular designer of the bear didn't think it would stand up to his dancing around. Of course they thought about all these things — afterwards!

'I did once have my own way. I had to get a man into a very complicated costume which was all straps and buckles and it was just impossible in the time. You couldn't do it. So I went to the director and told him so and he just said rather grandly: "Oh you'll have to do it, that's how I want it". In the end I said to him: "Well, you show me how then", and then he tried and of course he couldn't do it. After that the buckles were faked and put on top of press studs so that they just pressed on and it was all right, much more practical.

'I think the single funniest thing was when I was dressing Nicky Henson. He had an elaborate Elizabethan costume with a huge codpiece. It stuck right out. One night I tripped over something and to keep my balance I grabbed at the nearest thing to hand which was his codpiece. "Good God, Sybil", he said, "it might be all right on a dark night but not during a quick change. . . ." '

She says she enjoys the classics most — what she can see of them. 'I can never see a show all the way through, and because I'm working every night I can't see anyone else's either. For instance at the moment on matinee days we're doing what we call "back to backs", that is a matinee at 5 o'clock which finishes about 7.30 and then you are immediately on to the "half" for the next show. I never see any television either. It was better at the National because shows were in repertoire and you got some nights off.'

The most difficult show she has done, she says, was the National's *Guys and Dolls*. 'It was desperately hectic — everyone had dozens of costumes and constant quick changes. I enjoyed that particular show as I loved the music but I wouldn't like to do regular musicals — imagine coping with *42nd Street* every night.'

Actors become very attached to their dressers and ask for them time and time again. "I'm very lucky. I'm always in work. I'll have a letter from an actor or actress saying they are coming into town in a show at such and such a time and will I be free for them.

'A good dresser has to be alert and very, very responsible and you have to have a real understanding of your actor — in fact you have to be as one.'

Rob Barnard, deputy head of sound at the National Theatre, pictured in the Lyttelton Theatre.

The Sound Man's Tale

Sound in the theatre used to consist of a man standing in the wings making the sound of horses hooves with coconuts or banging a tin tray for thunder. Later a company might run to a record or tape for a few sounds — cars pulling up, seagulls, etc. Now it is far more sophisticated.

Rob Barnard is deputy head of sound at the National Theatre:

'I left school with very few qualifications, like one 'O' level, and I did become quite interested in technical theatre when I was at school and had quite an eye for the theatre, so that was my first experience. I knew from the word go that I didn't want to be an actor but I was interested in the "mechanics" of the theatre, lighting and sound particularly. So I left school and I worked around at odd jobs until eventually I discovered there were such things as drama schools and certain drama schools did technical courses. I applied for and got into the London Academy of Music and Dramatic Art (LAMDA). There was a technical and stage management course there which lasted two years. Whilst I was there I got to know quite a lot of people in the industry.

'At that time theatre sound was beginning to get quite interesting: there were some big new shows going into the West End, *Jesus Christ Superstar* for instance, which was the first big rock musical in a big West End theatre.

'In fact I worked on *Superstar* in my breaks from college because there was a tie up between LAMDA and Theatre Projects who were involved with the show.

'I left LAMDA and went to work with a repertory company in the Salisbury Playhouse in Wiltshire. I stayed there for a year — I was lighting and sound technician at the Playhouse, which was a wonderful experience if only for the fact that Salisbury is a beautiful city. Then, I left there and came back to work full time at Theatre Projects whom I had worked for in the summer breaks. One of the contracts I worked on whilst at Theatre Projects was the National Theatre, which at that time was in the stages of completion. Theatre Projects were responsible as consultants for the whole building, but the little bit of Theatre Projects that I worked for was responsible for installation of certain parts of the sound equipment. So I worked as a contractor in this building in 1974/5. Then I disappeared for a couple of years before coming back to work full time for the National Theatre. In the time that I have been here I have seen different technical engineering people come and go with different ideas, and different systems come in and been thrown out. I saw the very first one that was put in and the subsequent ones put in by other people. So I joined the National Theatre as a sound operator in about 1979.

'We have a certain hierarchy in the department. It's not very grand. I'm now deputy head of sound, but by having some kind of system it gives people something to strive for. You come in as sound operator, which means basically you are just responsible for the day-to-day running in the theatre — i.e., here we have a repertory system whereby the show is in for a couple of days, then that show goes out and another one comes in, next that one goes out, etc. Every two or three days we change round, so that person, the operator, would be responsible for changing round in each theatre the sound equipment. This may be anything from just moving a couple of loudspeakers on stage to fit in with the set, to putting in a complete rig of microphones and loudspeakers depending on what the play is; and the mixing console has to be changed accordingly for each play. So the operator who is responsible for that is also responsible for actually operating the shows in the theatre, sitting behind a console pressing the right button at the right time, pushing up the right fader at the right time — that is his main responsibility.

'The next stage up, if you like, is operator technician, which is similar but it means that you become slightly more responsible for the technical and the maintenance side of the equipment — i.e., maintaining it and recommending new purchases. We are very lucky here in that we are given quite a large budget in the sound department, not only for replacement of boring old paging systems which we also have to look after, but also for keeping apace of what is going on in the outside world, particularly in the recording industry: we have to come into contact with a lot of contemporary composers, producers and directors who are used to working in recording studios with big symphony orchestras or rock bands and expect to have this sort of equipment. We don't have all of it but we buy the bare essentials.

'We are also responsible for what used to be called the making up of tapes and what is now rather grandly called the 'designing' of the show! This means reading the script, going to production meetings — this is all happening before the first reading — and, if you are lucky, meeting the director before the production. If not, you may not even see him then. You may meet the director for the first time at the first read-through, which is always a bit embarrassing because there are loads of strange people all milling around and, if the director is strange too, he is slightly embarrassed as well and you have to make a bee-line and introduce yourself. . . .

'So you've read the script, got a few ideas, met the director and then you will try and pin the director down and have a talk with him about what he thinks he wants in the way of sound. Some directors like sound very much, value it, appreciate what it can do for their productions. Others think of it as a necessary evil and use it as little as possible and others look upon it as something they just have to have.

'One of the best people to work for soundwise is Michael Bogdanov: he is slightly outrageous but he has special effects that he loves. He loves the BBC thunderclap — there is a BBC thunderclap which you *always* hear — a marvellous effect, nobody has managed to get a better one. It's very, very old. We've also got a very good crash of plates and glass cracking, a colossal crash. Michael loves all these things — you see him rolling in the auditorium with mirth when we play some of the old-time favourites. He's not very subtle in his use of them but it doesn't matter. He likes funny buzzing, twanging-type noises which we end up using time and time again with slight variations.

'David Hare always comes with Nick Bicât, a contemporary composer who likes electric-type music and synthesizers. David Hare likes to have slightly filmic, very loud, very high-quality music and sometimes sound effects, but the sound effects have to be very subtle, very good quality, and he uses a lot of voice-overs — i.e., just voices in the background to amplify a scene. There was a scene in *Map of the World* that played particularly well. It went on up-stage, really too far back; but it had to be up-stage because of a change in scenery down-stage. It was too far away to be heard so we actually recorded a sort of little playlet on tape which they didn't bother to mime to; they were just standing there, looking as though they were in discussion, and you heard this rather good little playlet which we treated quite well. We put in an echo to make it sound as though it were in a corridor.

'Also in *Map of the World* there was a letter which someone was writing and we opened the scene with very loud, electric music that dipped down, and over that came Diana Quick reading a letter to somebody — a really nice moment. Of course in *Pravda* there was a lot of music, *News at Ten* type themes, crashing in very, very loud, very powerful. Richard Eyre is very similar. He likes music to punctuate. He uses Dominic Muldowney who is very well known now and he works here extensively. Richard likes to mix real musicians with tape, which is a thing they do quite a lot. Nearly every play here, almost without exception — *Duchess of Malfi* is the only one — uses live musicians, even if only for pre-show and scene change music; but I wonder just how many members of the audience realize it's live musicians and not just a tape because these guys are off stage in a studio somewhere and piped in. Looking after them is part of our job and quite a major one — making sure they come in on cue, balancing them up. If you have a band of instruments of different dynamics you have obviously got to balance them properly so that one instrument isn't too powerful and drowns out the rest.

'Peter Wood quite likes jokey sound effects: *On the Razzle* had quite a few whistles, bangs and hoots. We try and push Peter Wood during rehearsals "is there anything I can help you with. . . ." and he says "no, no, not now"; and then he will suddenly slip in during a note session at the previews and say we must have something in there, can we have it in ten minutes time and you have to run up and do it. To be able to do that is part of the challenge of the job: to run off and find church bells chiming or whatever it is within three minutes and to have it ready for the show that night. We have quite a large library, not of new records but of sound effects that we have accrued over the years.

'Now we'll look at two different plays. The first is *Love for Love*. When one reads the play there are in fact no sound effects in it at all other than a very vague reference to a clock tower and the time of day a couple of times. So, if you really wanted to, you could put in a couple of clock chimes, and Peter Wood said from very early on he did want them in. This was during the first read through which I attended which was, as I said, interesting but a little bit nervy because people didn't know what was going on and didn't know each other.

'Then came monitoring rehearsals — i.e., going in there, trying to catch the director before he started rehearsals or at the end of them or, in fact, during rehearsals, but just trying to catch him and see if he could come up with any ideas and whether he wanted me to do anything. It transpired, yes, there would be some clock chimes — he was quite specific — he wanted to tell the hour so it wasn't actually a chime of time, "ding, ding, ding", it was a "ding dong, ding dong, ding dong ding", which was half an hour or a quarter of an hour, and he wanted it to sound like a small city-type clock chime. Those were the instructions which I eventually achieved by cobbling some sounds together.

'It was also very obvious from the word go that music was going to be required, not only within the play — there is a scene at the end where there is a dance — but also a pre-show music for curtain up and scene changes. That was to be composed by Dominic again, which he duly did. However there was a limited budget on his show for musicians and Dominic wanted two violins and two woodwind, which he got; but he also wanted a keyboard. We couldn't afford a keyboard so we did something rather naughty — he actually recorded a keyboard and played the keyboard on tape. Basically you have a tape which has two tracks: one track has the music, that's the harpsichord, the other track has the beat; so the musicians play to the beat they hear on a pair of headphones and know they are keeping in time with the harpsichord. They have to wear headphones as the microphones they are playing into must not pick up the click. So Dominic recorded the harpsichord himself, as he has facilities at London University, and he just appeared on the morning of the technical rehearsal with a tape which we cut up.

'We use here things called broadcast type cartridges for replay of all our sound effects and music. They are similar to a cassette, but they are a little bit bigger. The machines in which you play them are very small so you can have lots of them in the control room, and the other advantage is that they are absolutely quiet in their operation so that when you go into the play and you push to start they are silent and you don't have the audience turning round saying "what's that noise". They are very convenient: as you have one effect per cartridge, and thus immediate access to that effect promptly on the machine — you don't have to wind tapes back to try to find the right sound effect. So there is always that job of having to transfer off the reel to reel tape on to a cartridge.

'Productions normally go: Saturday night finish the previous show, nothing on Sunday, Monday strike the old set and start putting up the new set, Tuesday carrying on the fitting up and a little bit of lighting, Tuesday night should start the technical which runs through Tuesday night to Wednesday, and now we try to go for a Thursday night public preview. On the Tuesday lunchtime, which is the only time we can get silence because of all of us hammering around, we have a band call where the composer will sit in the auditorium with communications via headphones to the bandroom and also communication to us in the sound-box, which is behind the audience, and we just run through the cues. He will have rehearsed the musicians prior to this, so at least they know what they are doing, and we just set approximate levels, each musician having his own microphone on which we can balance the level to feed out into the auditorium. Band call will last an hour and we will hopefully have got something useful by the end of it. If there are sound effects in the play you would also try and use a couple of minutes just to play those, to set some sort of level volume, because the director rarely listens to sound effects in the auditorium before the technical. He just appears at the technical and we try and sort it out there and then.

'From having done a band call and set a few levels we go into the technical on Tuesday night, which in the case of *Love for Love* is fairly straightforward — a few pieces of music which are easily scripted and then there is a dance at the end. Although at the time the musicians are still in the band room you have said to yourself "now what happens if Peter Wood wants to put the musicians on stage? and I bet he will — you won't be able to hear them, so you had better secrete some mikes on the set that they can play into should they come down onto the set''; which of course they do because, having worked with Peter Wood before, I realize he does that sort of thing at a moment's notice.

'We have covered ourself by putting a few microphones around the set at obvious points where the band might play, so fortunately it is a very smooth operation, and when Peter said ''it's not loud enough'' we could amplify it because there were mikes there. So that's *Love for Love*, and once we got into previews very little changed. With complicated shows with Peter Wood you can bet your life that the first preview is going to be absolutely nothing like the last preview. Everything changes drastically because he treats the preview period as a rehearsal period.

'That went on pretty easily really. Now *Yonadab* was a different kettle of fish. That was a *nightmare*. News of it was bandied about the building for many months before Peter Hall came to do it; and when you keep hearing about plays in that way, you know they are going to be a ''biggy'', you know they are going to be full of problems, especially if they are Peter Hall's shows, so we were all rather dreading it. However one of our team volunteered to take responsibility for it and he did all the right things by it: he had read the script, he tried to get a meeting with the director before the production meeting to no avail, he attended the production meetings and went into consultation with Dominic who again did the music.

'We knew that technically it was going to be quite complex. We knew that there were going to be musicians on a truck that could move up and down stage. This meant a cable from a moving truck on to the stage, and that also meant either some very canny self-paging cable device — i.e., as the truck moves down-stage the cable may pull up through a hole and then when the truck moves backstage it goes down the hole. Either it was that, which is what we subsequently ended up with, or it meant a man paging a cable all night, which is terribly boring and terribly extravagant. So we knew that, and that we had to have the truck and we knew we had to have the cable. At the time Peter Hall said categorically he did not want a cable in that truck, so we said okay we'll look at alternative ways of doing it knowing that we had to have these and microphones and also headphones on the truck where the musicians were. There are alternatives, including radio links, but we said really you don't want to get into that because it is very expensive and not one hundred per cent reliable. However, eventually Dominic managed to get Peter to change his mind.

'Peter's reasoning was that he was imagining some enormous great big white cable that would be visible from the back row of the stalls, which of course it wasn't at all — the truck was so far down that you could hardly see the truck let alone the cable. Anyway we got permission to use the cable, which was quite good, so we had the musicians on stage. We also knew that there were going to be some musicians hidden away in a room as well as in the studio, so that's "position musicians on truck and musicians in the room".

'We also knew that Dominic was at the time going to give a lot of recorded percussive sounds, drumming and so on, which is all computer generated — that is, real sounds but sampled by a computer, held in the computer's memory and then replayed. You can virtually replay the sound so, if you sneeze, that note is held in the computer and you can then play that sneeze with a keyboard. It's a device called fairlight and it's used a lot in pop music now. You can sample any kind of sound and then bend that sound, play with it and play it in stereo on the keyboard. That is what Dominic did with various sounds, very very clear. He spent many, many hours in the depths of the City of London University all night recording drum beats, drumming, and presenting us with tapes. Almost every other day we'd get another tape.

'So we knew Dominic was going to be doing this, we knew we had to re-play the tape into the house at very high, very good quality volume. We had the same problem keeping the two sets of musicians in synch [synchronized] with this tape — that is the musicians on the truck and the musicians in this room off — so they could all play together. We had to amplify the musicians in the room off and the musicians on the truck in order to bring them up to the level of the tape. We also had to amplify some of the dialogue for the chorus on the stage and the stage had to be miked as a whole.

'This is the sort of stuff that we knew we were going to be into fairly early on. Fortunately, the parameters within which we would have to work were fairly well defined. Exactly how they were going to work and how it was all going to come together we didn't really know, but that was what we knew we had: musicians in the truck, musicians off, and tape.

'Normally, as in *Love for Love*, you have a two-track tape — one track which is audio, the other is click for the musicians — whereas in the Olivier Theatre, where *Yonadab* was going to take place, Dominic wanted his music to be replayed in stereo. This means two tracks for the music and a third track for the click, which meant that you had to use a completely different machine to the one we had used for playback in the past. Now we also knew this from the word go, but nobody makes such a machine which is quiet enough to keep in the auditorium where the control is. So we knew we would incur another operator to operate that machine in another room off. As well as the guy in the auditorium at the mixing console who operates the tape machine, starts it and stops it, there was also the guy in the little room off who had to make sure that the tape was always in the right place when he went to start it again. We had to get up to three operators on that show — one on stage paging this stupid cable, one in the little room operating the tape machine and the real operator actually operating a mixer.

'And that, virtually, was how it ended up. It became so complicated for the main operator on the mixing console for two parts of the play (there is a very busy section in the second half) that there then had to be a second operator at the mixing console, so by now we are up to four operators on one show. The management at this stage were throwing their arms up in horror — they are normally used to one or at most, two. We covered ourselves pretty well because every time we knew we were getting into a situation where we were going to need extra personnel, which is extra money, we would go to the assistant director and say: "Listen we are going to need someone else and its going to cost whatever it costs to employ someone else. What can we do?" And he would say: "Go ahead, we'll sort it our later." This goes on all the time.'

How did the musicians manage on stage with headphones? 'They had to wear hats. Fortunately for us they were designed so they came down over their ears so that they were able to wear the headphones. They were listening to the clicks, but because they are wearing headphones they can't hear the dialogue on stage, yet they have to be able to hear the dialogue in order to play to it. So we had to feed them what's called show relay — which is the dialogue — into the headphones as well. They were in fact hearing three sounds: the click to keep them in time, the actual music which is on the tape, and the dialogues as well.

'It is terrible really because they sit on this little truck they can hardly move in, wearing very hot costumes, headphones clamped to their earholes — it's murder for them. It wasn't a very perfect experience for anyone. But if you are in sound then you have to be prepared for just about anything.'

Ian Williams, senior electrician for the Cottesloe Theatre.

The Lighting Designer's Tale

Theatre lighting began with candles. It progressed to limelight (using quicklime) then gas and electric footlights and finally to the complex masses of lamps we see now, most of which these days are computer controlled. It is no longer sufficient just to light the stage. Audiences, in part because of television, demand both subtle and exciting lighting techniques. Brian Harris is a freelance lighting designer who works both in this country and all over the world.

'I went into the theatre as an electrician. I went to the King Edward VI School in Stratford-upon-Avon and at Christmas they did a Shakespeare production so I worked backstage on that. Not particularly lighting but everything, and I became so interested that I applied for a place at the Royal Shakespeare Company when I left school. I waited about six months and then John Bradley interviewed me and I got a job as a trainee electrician — I think I was on about £7.50 a week then for a month's trial period and then I got the job. But my first real job was literally to make cups of tea. I started the first production Sunday of David Warner's *Henry VI*. In those days Peter Hall was married to Leslie Caron and I used to go and make cups of tea for them.

'John Bradley is a very good lighting man and very underestimated. He was very good within the RSC. He didn't do as much work outside the RSC but then there was a revolution in lighting around about twenty-five years ago and then computers came in in the seventies. Brad taught me a hell of a lot. I was very lucky and I was very keen. I think that was the biggest bonus because most people seemed less keen than me so I naturally got all the breaks. I was very lucky because the first year I was on tour with a Dramatic and Lyric Theatre Association (DALTA) season there was also a tour to Russia with Peter Hall's *Macbeth*, which I didn't go on but everybody else from the department did, or nearly everyone else. So that meant I was automatically the choice for the British tour which I did and it was very successful. I worked with Nick Chelton and would work out the lighting and put the rig up with the local crew and focus the lights and mount the show, as they were lit then by John Bradley and David Reed from the Aldwych. We took those all over the country.

'I had known that I wanted to do it myself from when I first sat down on that first day. I didn't realize that I would be any good at it but it was what I most wanted to do. Nor did I know how to do it.'

So how did he make the transition to lighting designer himself?

'I learnt a lot on all the small tours I did. I did the first Theatre-go-round *When Thou Art King* by John Barton, where I thought I was just operating the sound, but they wanted me to light it

as well — so that was my first show. That was a great success — not
the lighting — but the show. When I went to Japan and Australia
with the *Twelfth Night* tour, Brad lit *Twelfth Night* and *The Winter's Tale*
and went to Japan. Then I took it on and took both shows to Australia
on my own. After that I brought them into the Aldwych and from
then on my job was as assistant to Brad as lighting designer.

'So I coded the Romans in 1972 and did *As You Like It* as my first
main house show with Buzz (Goodbody). Then I did the Romans at
the Aldwych on my own and after that I was asked to go to The Other
Place. Meanwhile I had done other shows outside the RSC. Finally I
decided to leave the RSC in 1974, after doing the first two shows at
The Other Place, and chance my arm at freelance. It was a big step to
take because I had a good job at the RSC and early on I regretted it,
funnily enough, but now I don't because I've been lucky enough to go
all over the world several times and work on all kinds of shows, good
and bad.'

Presumably a lighting designer is in at the start of a production?

'Yes, I'm generally there when the set is being modelled up,
hopefully. I'm there then so that I can make changes at that stage to
help, but invariably there is too little time and the model is already
done. In either event we talk about ideas from there. It depends on the
director. Generally speaking I have found it's easier the second time
you work with somebody; the first time is quite difficult. But on every
occasion in my life, apart from one, I have worked with a director a
second time and that is almost true too of every show I have ever done
— I have always been asked back.'

So then he has to go away and work out what is needed?

'It's not always as simple as that. For example in the RSC there is
equipment inside an area which has to stay put for a whole season
because of the insane change-over situation at Stratford. So you are
lumbered from the very beginning at the RSC, but normally you can
put lamps where you want to for any particular show. You design
where you want to put the lighting; you make the decisions where you
are going to put them. Then you focus them. Then the day comes
when you have to put them into the computer. And you put in the
rather rough general stages, but always, always the show is late and
the lighting is the last thing that you put on and generally the one that
is under the most pressure, because we know what the set is going to
look like. The actors know their lines and the costumes have been
seen, but the lighting hasn't; and the lighting on the first preview is
invariably the weakest part of the show and it takes a lot of time to get
it right. But with computers of course it is easier to adjust. I mean on
some shows I would re-adjust during the preview. It's not often I do

that and I don't like it, but I have done.'

Lighting looks immensely complex now — it looks as if you could light a city with Stratford's lights.

'There are a lot. All the lights you see in the front of the house are for five shows and don't forget there is only an hour to change between matinee and evening — it's a big job. And of course in Stratford you are restricted. Immediately you undertake to do a show there your hands are tied to the established convention of the house. So there is only a certain amount you can do.'

What was the most complicated show he has ever done?

'I think it was a play called *Everybody Wants to Live*, written by Harold Levine, and it was very, very complicated in a sense that it depended on actors actually hitting precise marks on the stage every time or they would be in total darkness.

'If you go through a technical rehearsal properly — and there again I do have to say that the RSC tend to do a technical very well, sometimes spending two or three days on technical problem shows, which is good if it needs to be technically correct — then you are more likely to achieve your aim. Some other organizations don't, or think it's a big deal if you go on for more than six hours. But if you don't do the technical in as long as it takes then you end up with a disaster technically.

'You learn and you experiment and sometimes you suffer a lot because you just don't have time to get things experimented. You don't have time on stage.

'Good lighting now is a very subtle affair. There are a lot of things you do that the audience is not aware of which is good. The blase effects are quite crude and easy to achieve; the subtle things are a bit more difficult. You are restricted really with money, but I find it much more rewarding to do a show at the Everyman in Liverpool than doing a show at the RSC. Obviously in a prestige way the RSC is better. It's not to say that working in the RSC isn't the ultimate because the RSC does the best work in the world — there is no doubt about that in my opinion. But to light a show at the RSC doesn't require as much skill as working on a show in Liverpool with very young ASMs and technicians, because I find that in those places you are always working with enthusiastic people. They are less experienced, but then they make up for their inexperience by their enthusiasm. I have to say that I find when working in the bigger organizations that there is very often no enthusiasm, which is very sad, and that is why I prefer working with young people. You always get some reward from the work but it is *very* rewarding to work with young people. And it's good to work with no money, because when you do do the bigger shows you have much more experience in how best to buy and use equipment when you have had very little to use before — for example, at The Other Place as against the main house. Literally, everybody was against The Other Place at first and we had to steal items from the main house, literally steal them, because nobody wanted to give them or was interested, sadly, to begin with.'

How close is the liaison betwen lighting designer and sound?

'It depends on the show. Obviously I work very closely with the director and designer, although more so with the designer generally speaking and only sometimes with the sound, but it depends on the show. For example when I did *Dr Faustus* in Manchester I worked very closely with Adrian Noble, Bob Crowley and George Fenton but the sound operator not so much; but, on the other hand, I have just done *Wild Honey* in Denmark where the train sequence was very difficult, so then you work very closely with the sound people for hours and hours to get the whole thing absolutely right.

'It depends on the show really. But you must have the confidence of the director, for if he is not strong enough or doesn't trust you enough you can get into all sorts of trouble with technical problems. It's a very important time — the three or four days you have leading up to the first preview — and it is really dependent on the director. You feel very depressed sometimes when it's not finished or the director cuts you off and you don't have time to finish it properly. It depends on how the show comes out of the rehearsal room. If the shows come badly out of the rehearsal room then you can bet your bottom dollar that the technical side of the show will suffer, because the director will spend the technical time on stage with the actors rather than with the technical people.

'When the actors come up on the stage they should be in good nick as far as the performance is concerned, or we have "had it" anyway; but sometimes, sadly, the show comes out of the rehearsal in bad nick and the director desperately tries to put it right and therefore the other areas suffer as a result. And the time is consumed by the actors and the directors on specific problems of how they deliver lines or where they sit, rather than by musicians, technicians and designers.

'But when it does go right then, as I've said, it is very rewarding, the most rewarding thing there is. I wouldn't want to do anything else.'

Cicely Berry directing a RSC workshop for High School pupils in New York.

The Voice Teacher's Tale

Cicely Berry has a world-wide reputation as a voice teacher, a crucial role in the making of an actor. She has worked largely with the Royal Shakespeare Company but also outside it, including even work in prisons.

'I trained at the Central School of Speech and Drama as a teacher. While I was training I discovered a great deal of work was needed on the use of the voice. Mine was at that time very strong, but that was not enough. It's the emphasis on how you use your voice and on language (not in any precious kind of way) that is so important.

'You need to know how to "make" your voice both scientifically and physically, while remaining aware of the language and poetry, and of how we can use both in different ways. As I have always been absolutely obsessed with poetry — since I was about two and taught myself to read lots and lots of poetry — it was just something that I was particularly interested in, so it suited me very well. When I left Central I went and worked in some schools for a couple of years and then I went back and worked at Central and was responsible for the voice work of the acting trainees, because there were all kinds of students there — students training to be teachers, and others training to be actors, like Judi Dench and Richard Pasco who were there at the time I was; and there was a therapy department where people trained to be speech therapists.

'I worked there for about eight years full-time, training voices, working on the actual voice production, breathing and relaxation and all that, plus doing a lot of work on text, verse and working closely with the people who directed plays. While I was there there was this wonderful woman who was head of the school at that time, who's retired now, and who was very far seeing and had a great knowledge and vision about what work was, although not in any precious way. People used to come to her for lessons, people like Laurence Olivier used to go to her — a very high level of actors. She used to pass on to me people, actors, who wanted to work privately on their voices so I got a tremendous experience of working with people like Sean Connery and Peter Finch — one of my first people. I remember Finch was doing Iago with Olivier and that was why he came to me. Then Anne Bancroft, Topol — he came for accent mainly but he kept on for years and years — so I began to get experience with actors who were working in theatre as opposed to just training students.

'Then I had children and I left there so that I was only working part time and did much more teaching at home; later I opened my own studio for working actors in the West End and Drury Lane, and people used to come twice a week who were working nearby — lots of people used to come there.

'I also worked at that time with other people, like lecturers, people who spoke publicly but who were not able to communicate all that well. I remember one doctor who was very clever but had to lecture and just couldn't be heard beyond the first row. I remember several politicians came, like Philip Noel-Baker, even auctioneers from Tattersalls. I had this one auctioneer who was very, very bright but had a very strong cockney accent and he used to spend hours going "one-year-old foal, two-year-old foal"! He then ended up auctioning in front of the Queen. So I got a very wide experience of working. I also used to work a little bit with teachers and for the Ministry of Education.

'Then the job came up here [at the RSC] and I came to see Trevor and John Barton and they gave me the job. Now to begin with it was a very part-time affair, I think it was four days a week, and I did a lot of other work as well and it was mainly just to do with anybody who was not quite big enough for the big theatre and just to make sure that everyone was heard. That was on a one-to-one basis. For two or three years it stayed rather like that, but I did some group work with people who I actually wanted to work in that way though in fact it wasn't everybody who wanted to do it by any means.

'Gradually, through working with John Barton in rehearsals, I became much more in tune with what was happening and saw what was needed, shall I say. So I then started to work in rehearsals myself, at first just a little bit on scene, and then it grew and until the director became much more trusting. It's quite difficult to come and work on voices, as often directors tend to think that you are going to make people sound a little bit false — at least at that time they did. I hope that I have altered that attitude quite considerably although quite rightly they feel strongly that their work doesn't need to be interfered with.

'I suppose that lasted for about three or four years and gradually one was given total trust and actors wanted to work all the time, so now it's quite a different picture from when I first started.'

So what happens now? 'To begin with the work divides into three areas. One area is general voice work where I do general voice classes with as many people that can come, depending on rehearsals, just doing literally breathing and relaxation and quite a lot of language work. We take a lot of speeches from plays and just find out how the structure of the language works — how you can make it work physically with the breath and how you can move with it and how you can open it out by not concentrating too much on making it sound good but on feeling the language through your body.

'Then I go into the second part of my work which is specifically on each play in rehearsal and depends on the needs of that play and on its director. Some directors for instance work very naturalistically and therefore it makes it more difficult for the actors to perhaps honour the verse, so you have to try and aim for balance. Another director will go at it rather big and loud and fast, and you have to then take actors away and make them do it very quietly and think it through for themselves so that they can do the two things — they can actually be both very truthful to themselves and yet quite big in the way the director wants. So you find all sorts of ways of working which in the end achieves that balance. The difficult thing about Shakespeare for instance is the balance between being truthful in a naturalistic and modern way and yet being able to honour the verse and the imagary in it.

'I suppose one of the biggest influences on me was when Brook came here to do the famous *Midsummer-Night's Dream* and I worked very closely with him. He was oh so very specific about that. I went over to Paris and worked with him too; it's this continual trying to find the balance which is actually different really with every production you do.'

With the opening of the new Swan Theatre she now has the problem of Jacobean language that is not Shakespeare. . . . 'Yes, every text and even every Shakespeare play is different. Early Shakespeare is very formal and you have to find ways of breaking that formality up a bit, whereas in the late ones the verse gets broken in the middle of the sentence or is stopped in the middle of lines.'

Are there particular problems with actors who have concentrated on televison?

'Yes. The thing is they do a lot of TV and films in which they have to be very, very truthful in a kind of naturalistic way and then you start trying to make it bigger for the theatre and so they feel false. That is one of the major problems with actors that you have to work against: the fact that an actor has to feel true, and it isn't only that actors that have done a lot of television and film — it is also that our style of speaking has changed and our vocabulary. Our theatre has hopefully become less class conscious, it has less to do with a particular class and much more with the embracing of a different class structure. Therefore when you get good actors from the North you don't want them to lose their natural talent, natural energy or their natural truth that is their *own* truth. But they also have to discover a way of finding pleasure in the verse, because it was written as verse quite specifically and there is a wit and a meaning which comes out of the verse itself which you can't disguise. So it is actually giving them, the young actors in particular, a confidence that they can be big and can go with the extravagance of language without being forced themselves. It's finding the kind of energy that you get on a football ground really and translating that. I do a lot of work with schools, for instance, with young people and I do work in prisons, just on Shakespeare. Because I feel if we can get in touch with that language which is releasing feelings in a very articulate way which is not precious at all, then it makes people able to communicate much better. So I have also learned a lot from doing workshops in community theatres with quite rough kids. In December of last year I worked with High School kids in New York and at some of the more alternative schools, first making them excited with the language. It's influenced my work with actors a lot.'

A scene from the RSC's production of *A Comedy of Errors* for which Guy Woolfenden wrote the music.

The Composer's Tale

Music now plays an important role in the production of a play and many productions have it especially composed for them. Guy Woolfenden, music director of the Royal Shakespeare Theatre, is one of the most experienced and prolific.

'I think I first wrote for the theatre at Cambridge, where I studied music and one of my teachers was Raymond Leppard, who was the music adviser for the RSC, and he I think perceived that I had a theatrical flair and said it might be something that might interest me in the future. In fact I took up conducting and then, to earn a living, became a horn player for Sadler's Wells Opera as it then was, before it became English National Opera. I left to freelance as a conductor and eventually landed up here — I thought to stay just a year or two to conduct the orchestra.

'But then the first major project after I had been here about a year was the *Wars of the Roses*, that legendary production. It was postponed because Peter Hall had shingles or something and Raymond Leppard was by that time doing a revival at Glyndebourne and the dates clashed, so I suddenly found myself writing a major score. In my first year here I wrote music for everything anyone wanted.

'We used to have what were called studio productions in the conference hall which is now of course our new Swan Theatre. It has wonderful acoustics — what some people don't know is that it has some ancient peg boarding, acoustic boarding, round the shallow end. I was always told that it was a standby broadcasting studio in case London or Birmingham was ever completely bombed in the war. I wrote buckets of music for those studio productions, productions the public never got to see. We did studio productions with Michel Saint Denis and I wrote one or two scores. I did just the song for *Measure for Measure* which starred Judi Dench. . . and I did, looking back on it, an appalling score for a production of *Julius Caesar*. But I think they obviously saw that I had some talent outside that of being music director, part of whose function is to be able to edit and re-write, change music if the composer is unavailable, and I suddenly found myself overnight appointed musical director because my predecessor Brian Priestman left to pursue a conducting career.

'I also found out the same night, as we were in the middle of one of our then perennial financial crises, that my band of musicians which was fourteen strong had been decimated to about half that; and so we had to find a new way of doing music which was a sort of visual-oral approach. You could obviously hear them but you could also see them. They dressed up in costumes and rehearsed as carefully as the actors and played from memory a number of instruments that could perhaps be authentic but at least they didn't worry their minds about that visual aspect. I did the whole series of the *Wars of the Roses* and added *Richard II* and *Henry IV* parts one and two. I started from the history plays with their many battle fanfares and slowly eased my way into the lyric plays and found I had a taste for it, although I still find it just as difficult, in fact more difficult than ever.

'I have to think very quickly when a show is going up in an half-and-a-half — it's happened to me three times in the last ten days because we are still discovering how to make the Swan work. Exits and entrances keep changing and scene-change music you didn't think you needed has to be added, lengthened, shortened or whatever; so under those circumstances I can react and produce something very quickly. I actually like to live very dangerously although it drives me nuts as it must do my wife and the directors. Obviously if there is a song or dance that the actors have to learn I try not to deliver that late, but incidental music — which may be only incidental to the British public — is to me highly important because it can set the mood and tone and character. I tend to leave that pretty late because I think the play develops enormously in the last two or three weeks of rehearsal. If you went away and wrote it two months before the production opened you would find the ground had shifted under your feet and what you thought you were doing is no longer relevant.'

How about a show which is heavily reliant on music like the Trevor Nunn *Comedy of Errors*?

'That comes into the category of "if you've got songs and dances you have got to get them in early". That is not to say they were in early because, although Trevor Nunn is now one of the most sought-after directors of musicals in the world bar none, that was his first absolute out-and-out musical. He had been nudging towards it for years in his approach to several plays like the second Act of his *Winter's Tale*, with Judi Dench, which had in those days a sort of contemporary rock score. I don't think even Trevor with his experience now with *Starlight Express, Chess* and *Les Miserables*, knew exactly what was involved. I certainly didn't. It was only the second or third musical that I had attempted. What we are really talking about is the time-span of writing musicals. I was very relieved to hear that Leonard Bernstein, with all that talent and all that experience on Broadway, took from day one to the first performance of *West Side Story* something like two years. *The Comedy of Errors* I had two or two-and-a-half months warning about before the company assembled for the season. They then had four or five other productions to put together and we were still writing numbers as we went into rehearsal, you know burning the midnight oil.

'Some of that was enjoyable, some of it is just sheer hard work. But to get back to a score for a Shakespeare play — I try and get the songs in early; otherwise it is not fair to the actors. Dances, too, or at least the dance rhythm if not the actual melody. But for incidental music I think you should soak up what the production is all about, that's the first priority. The other thing I was going on to say is that you don't actually know, as you do when you are writing television scores, the timings of anything until you actually start what we laughingly call the "tech". We have just been "teching" two new productions and we have also been "teching" the building as well so it has been doubly difficult. We have adjusted music, lighting, lines, cutting lines back in and out every single day.

'You have to be adaptable. Although you should fight quite hard for things you believe in and lose only after a struggle with the director, you mustn't think the music is any more or less important than, say, the lighting or the costumes. Certainly it isn't as important as the acting, although it is incredible what, subliminally, the music can do to a play and you can only find this out, as the actors will tell you, when you do a run through without any music. When the director wants to run the whole scene and the familiar exit-entrance music which helps to twist the play's plot, delineates time, space, distance, events, when that is removed from them, they will tell you how much it means to them and the audience picks this up too. I say subliminally not in terms of its volume, which can be quiet or loud depending on the sensitivity of the scene following or preceding.

'It ceased to bother me twenty years ago whether people say "Oh wonderful music" or not. Sometimes the fact that they say nothing at all means that it has worked. Sometimes it shouldn't stick out like a sore thumb, although it is always very pleasant when people do notice it and like it, but its function is not the same as it increasingly is in some popular films with their huge budgets. It's not there for the film to be repeated so many times that you can't fail to go out whistling it and you buy the LP. That is not the purpose of theatre music. It has a much more serious function.'

Does he choose which plays go into repertoire?

'Oh no. I can choose which plays I do *not* want to do. I'm on the planning committee so I am part of the debate which is obviously essentially a function of our directors to which I contribute. If there is something I particularly hanker after I unashamedly go and lobby a particular director and say "I'd love to do the scores for you if you'll have me", but they have absolute total freedom — I am there to advise.

'I am also extremely proud of the fact that over the past five, six, seven years I have pushed with great conviction composers who have never worked for the RSC before on to directors who are very, very timid about a new face and someone that they have never met. They would sooner go to the devil they know than a devil they don't. I'll give you one particular case, that of a young lady composer with the amazing name Ilona Sekacz, although I'm not claiming to have discovered her. She first wrote to me almost twelve or thirteen years ago when she hadn't actually fully developed into a composer but had developed into a very interesting person with ideas about musical theatre and techniques of singing. I did in fact interview her then and I said the usual thing, and meant it, "keep in touch", and she did keep in touch. She sent me an amazing sort of singing guide, a sort of musical version of the wonderful work that Cicely Berry does, just at the time when Adrian Noble was getting right into his stride and doing major productions like *King Lear*. He wanted a new composer and at one point I thought, well I could do all the sort of dog's-body work, so let's have fanfares instead of music; but I had a kind of dream that the way to do the story was vocally and I thought that perhaps I could get Ilona in to work on that side of it and excite Adrian over it. He was excited but very nervous. Ilona on the other hand was bounding with confidence and didn't want me clouding the scene, virtually saying "either I do it all or not at all". Her success with that score was such that she is now certainly into double figures with the Royal Shakespeare Company and that goes for other people too.'

Did he, for instance, discover George Fenton?

'No. He was introduced to the RSC by Peter Gill long before he was famous for *The Jewel in the Crown* and *Gandhi* when he did *Twelfth Night* and that was when I first met him. I was very impressed then and I did all I could to encourage him. Composers like Stephen Oliver first came to us in almost the same way as Ilona. I heard of him as a phenomenon who had written hundreds of operas when he was in his teens at Oxford and he came to us through Keith Hack when he did an amazing production of *Measure for Measure*. I then gently pushed him in the direction of Trevor Nunn. . . . The one I'm proud of most recently is Jeremy Sams who has been appointed as music director with the regional tour which went out last year with *The Crucible* and *The Winter's Tale*. I have seen enormous skill, talent and theatrical flair there. I'm not old but I've started feeling old, because it could have been me fifteen or twenty years ago. I even discovered very late in the day that we went to the same school in Croydon and the same university and therefore had some of the same teachers yet we couldn't be more different in other ways.

'After Bill Alexander and I had collaborated on *Richard III* (I think it was my third *Richard III*) he said he wanted to do a 1959 *Merry Wives of Windsor* and he wanted me to arrange the music. Now I am much nearer 1959 than Jeremy Sams and it clashed with the Young Vic who were putting on the musical *What a Way to Run a Revolution*. I completely supported Bill's seemingly crazy idea because it is one of the few Shakespeare plays you can update as, apart from Falstaff, there are no lords or ladies, kings or queens but real people in a real environment. A lot of people were very critical of the update but I totally supported it and I was very sad I wasn't able to do it. Once again Bill was understandably anxious about taking on board a totally unknown composer in only his second main house production after *Richard III*, but they hit it off so well together that they are now collaborating at this very moment on a *Midsummer-Night's Dream*.'

Did he never feel that he wanted to do an opera?

'Oh yes — there is a world elsewhere! Over the last five or six years I have increasingly tried to compose one or two works which either have nothing to do with Stratford or the theatre, unless they were initially inspired by working here. For example, I have written an oboe concerto and a clarinet concerto and a huge piece for a military band, or what we now call a concert band, which is a huge movement in America where there are 60,000 of them. I've been writing for wind bands all my life because Stratford is basically a wind band to which we sometimes add strings.

'But I still get my biggest thrill as a performer. I'm not an actor but I do have that hankering to appear and perform, and as a conductor I more than keep my hand in. I run two orchestras as artistic director — I always ditch them, and they know that I'm going to, if it clashes with an RSC production week or whatever and I conduct opera whenever I can. I did three productions with the Scottish Opera. You ask if I write operas: well at least I do the next best thing, as I recently adapted, yet again, *The Beggar's Opera* for an opera company rather than an actor company. There are only two ways to do *The Beggar's Opera*: you either do it with actors who can't sing or singers who can't act, and the search has been on for hundreds of years to find that strange animal which exists increasingly, I'm glad to say, who can both sing and act; and I would fight a duel to the death with anybody who said that our Macheath couldn't do that. I think he is one of Britain's finest actors/singers and I don't just mean singers, I mean he is one of the finest baritones in the whole world, namely Tom Allen, whose notices recently for the Busoni *Faust* were marvellous. He is quite an extraordinary man and when we were having trouble with the production and we felt the glint of steel behind the back, he remained loyal and true to the end. When we performed it in

Newcastle on tour with his local audience it was quite amazing because he is a Geordie. It was like Joe Johnson beating Steve Davis at snooker.'

Sean Baker (facing camera) as Danceny and Alan Rickman as Valmont in the fight scene from *Les Liaisons Dangereuses*.

The Fight Director's Tale

Good fights do not just happen in the theatre. They are very carefully designed — not least to ensure nobody gets hurt. Malcolm Ranson is one of the country's leading fight directors. How did he start?

'Well, really it goes back to my school-days. I think I had always been a bit of a romantic. I enjoyed watching the old Flynn movies, although I suppose I didn't see all that many when I was young, but I do remember being taken in to a cinema — not to actually watch the film — but because I was with an aunt who was going to meet someone and they were showing *Captain Blood*. I was absolutely mesmerized by the costume and the wonderful ships they had and I suppose that started the interest in the sort of romantic period look. Then I began going to the cinema and seeing some of these romantic films with sword fighting. After that I used to play sword fights in the streets, stealing bamboo canes from people's gardens to use as swords and then a teacher arrived at school who wanted to start a fencing club and I was in like a shot. I thought "right I'll do that".

'I must have been about thirteen at the time and I started fencing at this club, which didn't last for very long because it wasn't very professional. Fencing is the sort of sport that you really have to learn properly — you cannot just pick it up, it's not like kicking a ball around. But I was keen enough to persevere and because the club had actually folded at school the teacher said: "Look, there is a place in town — if I can get your parents' permission I'll take you along". And that is in fact what happened. So right the way up to leaving school at eighteen I did modern fencing as a hobby. Then at college, when I trained as a drama teacher at Bretton Hall, I taught the students how to fence and did fights in various shows, after which I went back to my home town and taught for three years, also working as an amateur, acting or directing and putting fights in shows.

'Then I gave that up to go into the theatre proper, starting at the Young Sheffield Playhouse which is no longer there; really while I was there it was a question of "can anyone fence? — "I can" — "well you do the fights", and it started like that. So I was an actor who occasionally directed fights in shows. Next I moved to London and I worked on a show with the then National Theatre fight arranger Bill Hobbs, and I looked after the fights for him — he couldn't make all the rehearsals because of his commitments at the National. About four or five months later I bumped into him again and I was doing another show at Greenwich and he said: "What do you do after this?" I said: "I'm going to be unemployed." He said: "Well, look I've got some freelance fights coming up which I am going to turn down because I don't have the time to rehearse them so, if I plot them, can you rehearse them for me?" "Certainly," I said. It was an opportunity not to be thrown away.

'So for a number of years I worked with Bill on those shows as his assistant. I would also act in shows in my own right. For a while I didn't know what I was: I was a sort of actor who did fights, who worked with Bill as his assistant, until slowly it evolved over the years that more and more fights kept coming my way and fewer and fewer acting jobs. If you like, the fights took over and it reached a point where I had to decide what I was. So I decided to go with the fights game. It was a long apprenticeship over a number of years, not taking a conscious decision at the time. This happens to most fight arrangers — they probably start off as actors but have an interest that slowly develops over the years.'

So is stage fighting now taught regularly at Drama Schools?

'It varies. There are more drama schools teaching both armed and unarmed combat now and stage fighting. Sometimes you do get actors who haven't touched a sword in their life or even done a fight. If you are very, very lucky — which can be wonderful — you get someone who has been trained and at least has a basic background knowledge. Then you are half way there because if you are working on *Romeo and Juliet*, a lot of the time is just teaching someone how to hold a sword, how to move, how to handle themselves. Whereas if they have already got that background knowledge then you can go on to actually plotting the fight and working at it.

'It's a violent dance routine, that's the easy way to describe it: every hand movement and every foot movement is worked out to the finest detail because you cannot ad lib a sword fight. You can make up words if you forget them, but obviously you cannot do that in a sword fight — it's far too dangerous. It does require a great deal of rehearsal and not everyone appreciates the amount of time it takes actors to do the sword fight. Some directors say that they want you for a certain period, and give you plenty of rehearsal time; other directors who may not know anything about fights think you can go in, give them a few minutes, then go away again. Somehow the actors will do it. There are even some directors around in some of the Reps, who think: "Oh well, let the actors work it out for themselves". That can be very dangerous.

'There are a number of frightening stories. I believe, in a schoolboys' production in Manchester (this goes back quite a number of years and I don't know the full details), one of the swords broke and passed through the body of one of the actors and actually killed him! You do hear all sorts of stories, mainly from the past because we are more educated nowadays, but not completely, and it is still considered in certain theatres that fight directing is an extravagance. I suppose a lot of it is financial. They think: "Oh well we'll get the local fencing master or one of the actors to do it or someone with a little knowledge in the company, or I've done a bit, I'll do it" — that isn't enough experience, you need someone who knows more than that.'

Are actors protected in any way in stage fights?

'No, not at all. The swords are obviously blunt but they are still potentially dangerous. The only way you can make them safe would be to give them rubber swords but that would look ludicrous because they would bend and waver in the breeze. . . . As soon as you do fights on stage you are asking the audience to believe in the reality of the true fight, and you are asking the actors not to hit each other. So you try to make the fight as safe as possibly by fighting "out of distance" for thrusts. Certain moves have to be "in distance" because if you take a cut and the actor avoids it by ducking down, you have to be close enough to him in fact to really have been able to hit him or look as if you were going to hit him. It's no use him being four feet away and you giving a swish and him ducking. The other thing is that the sort of weapons you use have to take a great deal of punishment because they have possibly to go through a four- to eight-week rehearsal period, in use every day, being hit, bashed, thrown around, dropped on the floor. Now if you use wooden swords or some sort of alloy swords they don't last very long, so the best material is still steel made blunt. But a steel sword can give you a very nasty crack or, if you get the point of it in a vulnerable part of the body, it's not going to do you any good. So the requirement of stage fights call for a tremendous amount of discipline, control and rehearsal.'

The manner of fighting has altered down the centuries too, so the fight arranger has to adapt. 'Absolutely. Because as you go through the history of combat it changes from what was basically bashing on the head, then somebody bashing you, to the development of the swords and your handling of it as it became more scientific as a weapon. There are so many different styles of weapons. You would wear a different sword in the streets to the one you took to battle with you. So weapons change throughout the periods of history. You had the large broadsword with a straightforward cross hilt, and from that you would have the big two-hander which is an enormous weapon. Then you had the rapier — basically a piece of round steel ground to a point which you used for ramming into people. Then you get the court sword of the eighteenth-century which is a very delicate, fine blade used mainly for point work. During Shakespeare's time it was the rapier, rapier and dagger, rapier and buckler, all sorts of different weapons. You can never be totally specific and say this weapon is this period: it would be ludicrous to say that in the 1960s everyone wore a mini-skirt — they didn't. So, also, in the carrying and use of weapons there would be overlaps in style. There would always be more than one sort of weapon. You would still have rapiers at the same time as you had court swords or small swords; and you wouldn't carry a small sword to battle with you, you would want something that was much much sturdier and more lethal, like a sabre, something with which you could easily chop off heads. So, the style of fighting depends on the sort of show you are doing and on the period in which it is set.'

So taking, say a production like the National Theatre's *Coriolanus* (in which Ian McKellen played the leading role) presumably fight rehearsals start as early as the main production rehearsals?

'Yes, I worked with Ian and Greg (who played Aufidius) right from the beginning because there was a good deal of discussion as to the period we were setting the play in. It was a little ambiguous. It began in modern suits and then went virtually — but not quite — into Roman togas. Certainly a lot of the battledress had a hint of the Roman period with its angular breastplates and the style of helmets. When considering the weapons, we knew we had to use swords at some point as there are so many references to them. We also thought we would use spears, too. They were going to be standing around with pennants on them first, but we decided that would not work, so we honed it down to swords and shields for the fights. But what kind of sword? We decided to use a light form of sabre which even modern-day soldiers wear as a dress weapon so that you would still have a link with today.

'Although we don't use shields today it was decided we would have to, and to hell with it if people thought it anachronistic as they had so much flexibility. We also wanted to have the real sound of the fights. You see, in the theatre, swords don't make the kind of sound people think they make. All the sound on films and TV is dubbed on afterwards so you get the clashing sounds and the ringing noises and people panting and grunting and so on. Shields in the past weren't always made of steel; they were often made of wooden boards covered with hide and just the edges rimmed with steel or bronze. A huge iron shield would be too heavy to fight with. I saw a perfect example of that in an awful film about Vikings called *The Norsemen*. The only thing that looked authentic was the boat. The costumes were unbelievably dreadful and the shields were all metal. In real life they would have been wood but of course wooden shields instead of going "boooooooiiiinggg" would just go thud, which is a dead sound.

'So for *Coriolanus*, with just two people fighting in a gladiatorial pit, we actually got the armoury department to create special metal shields. They were heavy for the actors but each shield had a handle and a strap and a special metal bar which linked the two; then there was a piece of metal which the shield went on to so that it was like a bell. So the actual connection between the bell part of the shield and your grip was just one central point and when you hit it, it actually went "booooooiiiinggg". It made a terrific sound. We hung a mike in as well and put a little echo on it so that you had an actual clash of steel on steel which sounded as it does in the cinema. . . .'

What was the most difficult fight he had directed? 'Always the next one, I suppose. . . . But there are certain fights that are more complicated to work out. For instance the one in *Les Liaisons Dangereuses*. Now that is one of the best plays I've ever seen. We had added problems with that one which come about when you do a fight in a small space like The Other Place, and with an audience on three or four sides. You not only have to devise a fight where the actors don't hit each other but ensure too that they don't hit the audience either. You can't just put them in the middle and have them stand still and go tic, tic, tic, tic, with the swords. You have to have a fight which utilizes the space but also makes the audience feel secure.

'That particular fight was complicated by the fact that you had to show the feelings of those taking part. It's easy in a script to say things like: "Valmont only just parries this move because he is disorientated at that time, thinking of Madame so-and-so, etc. . . ." Obviously you can't say in a fight, "now this is where he is thinking about this", or have a voice over, so you have to do it without dialogue. Valmont, in this story, actually allows his death to happen and that's very difficult without someone just saying "kill me", in the middle of the fight. So you had to go through a progression of what happened so that the audience becomes aware of it instead of it being obvious. I worked on it with Ilona Sekacz in creating moments within the fight where there could be sound references back to previous events and where Valmont, obviously the better swordsman, could show his distraction by making a move and not completing it, walking away from the fight. There is one moment of indecision when you think he's going to walk on Danceny's sword but he doesn't, he knocks the blade up and the fight starts again. He does a similar thing later and then changes his mind and backs away, then he tries to provoke him by knocking the sword and provoking him again which actually leads to the moment when he no longer defends himself and says, without words, fight me, fight me, kill me NOW. . . . Yet it must not look as if Danceny is killing him in cold blood because that is not what happens. We must not make Danceny look like a villain or that he is doing a cowardly dirty deed. He kills Valmont because Valmont suddenly leaves himself open to be killed.

'I was very lucky with the actors. Alan Rickman (Valmont) had done a lot of fencing before but Sean Baker (Danceny) had done very little; then suddenly he had to do what is probably one of the most complicated sort of fights.'

Not all fights are serious. The fight in *The Critic*, for example, is ludicrous and done to music — *Rule Britannia* in fact. In *The Twin Rivals* there was a fight between a good swordsman — who took his coat off and folded it up while fighting — and a bad one who tried to do the same thing and ended up with it wrapped around himself so that he tripped over it.

'The other thing that worries me, certainly as a fighter/actor at times, is that you can work with actors that have never done a fight before and they can be wonderful in rehearsals but you don't know how they are going to react in front of an audience. The first time in front of an audience is always a worrying time for the fight director because, although you have rehearsed the moves, you have to explain: — "don't ad lib, even if you have to say to each other 'what do we do next?' Go off, or just die because you are meant to die. Don't ad lib a fight whatever you do." Obviously some actors are more nervous on stage. It comes out in various ways: the knees can go, they can tremble, they can do all sorts of things, but it's like a new form of discipline doing it on stage for the first time. Some actors come through it with flying colours and some actors go to pieces at one point. Then panic sets in, and usually if they just stop and then get back into it you know they have crossed that barrier and they are going to be all right.

'*Hamlet* is different again. You've got this strange situation where the actor playing Hamlet has gone through some of the most emotional, draining, philosophical soliloquies — a whole evening, which can be three, three-and-a-half hours and then it comes: "Oh my God, we've got the big fight to do". You've got the actor playing Laertes who considers his whole performance is the fight. He's been sitting around doing nothing all night and he's coming on raring to go and Hamlet's wishing it was all over! So, a tricky situation — one actor emotionally and physically drained, and another actor fresh and ready to show the world his Laertes.'

What happens if there have to be a number of fights? With *Romeo and Juliet* coming up, does this pose special problems?

'Yes, major battle scenes or a mass fight pose their own problems and require a discipline in (a) working them out and (b) for the actors performing them. Because you are working on an individual number of fights in a space, you have to worry not only about the actors who are fighting each other, but also about the other actors who are fighting close by to them. If you are fighting with ruddy great swords you see the actor in front of you whom you are fighting but you may not see the little guy coming up behind involved in his fight. The fight has to be worked so that they are not going to collide with each other and that is very tricky to do because it requires absolute positive discipline on everyone's behalf, working as a team; it just needs one person out of synchronization and the whole thing can fall apart. People can get too close to other people or not be at the right place at the right time. You cannot say "this is your area, stick to it", because it would just be lots of individual fights going on in different parts of the stage; so what you try to do is create situations where a particular fight takes a particular route — as that fight moves out of that space this fight moves into it and maybe somebody gets hurt in that fight and joins another fight. So instead of it becoming one against one it becomes two against one for a certain amount of time. In fact your focus of stage is changing and that is very, very complicated to do.

'When we did *The Scarlet Pimpernel* (which was on at Her Majesty's) it was fine while we were doing it at Chichester because it was one spacial area. Then it went on tour before it went to Her Majesty's and it was playing theatres with small stages, tiny stages, big stages and you had full company on there fighting. OK it's a comic fight, it's a silly fight but some of them had swords, some staffs, some knives, and that was a problem — having to adapt to different size stages at every venue they played in.'

Malcolm Ranson is a very busy man. He was working on *Romeo and Juliet*, a new play in Manchester and *Carmen Jones* at Sheffield, where actors have to appear to be boxers and where fights are with fists or knives outside the ring. This involves other problems like actors making their own sounds during punch-ups so that they sound like cinema fights.

'I went back to trying to be an actor a few years ago but after a while the parts dried up. That doesn't happen with fight directing. I'm so busy I've got to the point where I wake up, wonder where I am and then think: "Oh, it's Tuesday — this must be Sheffield!" '

'Take Back Your Mink', from the National Theatre's production of *Guys and Dolls*. This is the 1983 cast. The musical numbers were staged by David Toguri.

The Dance Director's Tale

David Toguri was born in Canada and went to school there before going on to study dance. 'I worked in ballet at home and then went to New York. I worked in stock for *years*. You just couldn't get any work then if you were an oriental, unless it was an oriental show. Nowadays of course it doesn't matter. Anyway, finally I got myself into an oriental show in New York and came over to England with that in 1960.

'I went back and forwards for a time — I did a Sammy Davis Junior show and while I was in it Madame Rambert saw me and asked me if I would like to actually choreograph something. It was called *Collaboration* and it was just that, a collaboration between dancers and designers from one of the big schools. I felt I had nothing to say choreographically and told her so, but we talked and talked and she kept on encouraging me and in the end I agreed to do it and that's how I met the designer, John Napier. Anyway we did the ballet and it got very good reviews, although when I say ballet it was actually more of a dance drama than conventional ballet.

'Next the La Mama Theatre came over here with *Hair* and I was taken on as an assistant. That way I became involved with the director who was himself very involved with dance and that's how I found myself working with actors.'

From *Hair* he began working in the Reps — with people like Jane Howells. 'Then I worked with Robin Phillips and Richard Eyre and it was when Richard came to the National Theatre that he asked me to do some work for them. He rang me up one day and told me he was going to do *Guys and Dolls* and would I like to choreograph the dances for it, which was wonderful as I thought it was a terrific show. So I found myself working at the National Theatre.'

Dance and movement are now major parts of a production. Actors, like dancers, are expected to work out and warm up. 'It's hard for them but it's fun. It's like a game and I get them doing all kinds of things to get them ready for what comes next — races, bouncing balls, skipping, follow-my-leader. All these things I find very good as the actors get tuned in to the same wavelength and that's necessary because some might be fantastic natural dancers while some have very real difficulties. The problem is getting them to meld and to make sure they feel a real commitment to a song or dance. So they have to do a good deal of that kind of work.

'Next I see what they are best at and start working on that as we begin to develop a body language for the number or routine. With *Guys and Dolls* we started off by doing lots and lots of different walks to put over the different characters, and then we started doing the walks to the music. We did tap dancing every day — the simplest tap — but they were really very good at it and it was important because it gave them a sense of rhythm. Then we moved on and made it more stylized and more individual to them and this was necessary too because none of them were actually dancers.

'But you are not working on all this on your own. What you are doing has to be within the style of the production. I've always seen the work of a particular director first so I know how he works and what he likes. I don't like to impose on a production, so it's no good my working out a fantastic dance routine which is then totally out of place. It's quite a complicated matter. A dance routine has not only got to follow the style of that particular production: it has to progress smoothly out of what has happened before and progress just as smoothly into what happens next — it has to meld right in and meld right out.'

At the time I saw him he was working on a production of Brecht's *The Threepenny Opera* for the National Theatre, which of course is based on John Gay's *The Beggar's Opera* which the National has also put on in the past. 'I started out by carefully reading the text. I've used the text to do all the dance numbers. For instance, in the famous tango between Macheath and Jenny you know the two of them are playing games. Jenny has just told the police she knows where Macheath is as she is bitterly jealous because she realizes he's after someone else. So I try to put into that tango the power game being played out between these two people and which can develop their characters as well — all part of the show.'

Not all the work he does is in the form of set dances. For instance in the Royal Shakespeare Company's production of *The Tempest* he had to devise a Masque, work with Ariel on the movement for the show, choreograph a dance for some nymphs and shepherds and work out a nightmare sequence of strange and weird creatures which were all part of Prospero's magic. 'One of the most difficult Shakespeare productions I've done was the RSC's *Midsummer-Night's Dream* with the puppets. We never really solved that, never knew whether the puppets were supposed to be the fairies or were being manipulated by the fairies — but it was fun, although really very difficult.'

Most difficult of all, he says, is opera, especially opera at the big international opera houses because of the extremely old-fashioned way they work. 'It's not just because opera singers have big egos — I think you have to have a big ego to star in grand opera — but it's not having enough time to work on the dances properly. You are lucky if you can get one hour a day. The big stars fly in and just do that one role that they are doing all over the world in different productions. Once you have got as far as the dress rehearsal you aren't allowed to change anything even if you don't think it works. It's really weird.

'It's not too bad when they use ballet dancers because at least they are used to dancing, but it is very difficult indeed to work with the singers when you get so little time, just an hour or so here and there.'

Working on a show with a big theatre company is very different. 'I get full mornings to rehearse with the cast; then I work on individual pieces during the day. For *The Threepenny Opera*, for instance, I'm working solo with Macheath, who is played by Tim Curry — I've known Tim a long time, in fact I got him his Equity card! — and then I work with the gang, then the whores and so on. Working with actors is a very specialized field, — there's not all that many of us who do it. I think both Gillian Lynne and I have a feel for it. It's a far cry from the old days in the theatre. Big stars were more like the opera singers today, coming in to do their *Hamlet* or *Richard III*. The drama schools only did the most basic work on dancing and singing. If you put on *As You Like It* for instance, you'd hire a tenor to sing the songs. Nowadays you expect to have several actors in a company who can sing well and a number who have a feel for dance. Some actors are extremely acrobatic.

'Working with actors can be frustrating but it is also very rewarding. They put a tremendous amount into it. They tell you if they don't like something and that's good. It's no use trying to force something on to them if they can't do it. Then again they can say to you "I don't think this character would do this or do it at this point" and then you stand back and look at it again and usually agree. I see my job as encouraging actors to put all their talents into what they are doing, to bring out the very best that particular person can do in that particular role — I find it fabulous.'

Clare Venables, Director of the Crucible Theatre.

The Crucible Theatre, Sheffield

What strikes you forcibly about the Crucible Theatre is that it is full of life. For twelve hours a day it is open to the public and it is a focal point of city life. Also noticeable was the enthusiasm of all those involved for what they were doing. Time and again I was told by Crucible employees that not only were they lucky to be working; they were more than lucky to be working at the Crucible.

The theatre opened in November 1971 and it cost £875,000. The name was chosen in a competition. A crucible is a melting pot and a form of crucible is used to make steel which, when the theatre was built, was Sheffield's flourishing traditional industry. Alas, this is no longer the case.

There are two 'theatres' within the building. The biggest seats 982 (although this can be increased to 1,013) with the audience seated on three sides around a thrust stage. The stage is extremely flexible. It is made in sections so that any part of it can be removed, while the above stage lighting comes from a grid known as the 'egg crate' because it looks rather like an egg box.

The Studio Theatre is basically a 50-foot by 50-foot space with two galleries. It seats 250 and the seats can be arranged in any way. They can be on three sides, diagonally, each side with the 'stage' area in traverse, or conventionally with the 'stage' at one end and all the seats facing it. They can even be removed all together.

There is a large foyer and people are encouraged to use it even if they are not going to the theatre. There is a restaurant which offers a 'shoppers lunch', a coffee and snack bar, a drinks bar and a shop. There is comfortable seating where you can meet a friend for a chat over a cup of coffee.

Compared to many theatres outside London and certainly to the small fringe houses and groups, the Crucible is very well supported by in-house workshops. It has a large one for making all the sets and big props and a separate Prop Shop, a medium-sized Wardrobe Department and separate departments for lighting and sound. There is a rehearsal room and a Green Room for staff. Front of house staff include a full-time manager and a well staffed box office. There is a proper Marketing, Press and Publicity Department. On the administration side there is the theatre's administrator, a financial controller and a casting and research person. The overall director is Clare Venables and her associate director is Mike Kay. There is no permanent resident company but the Crucible does tend to draw on a 'pool' of actors that are known to the directors and who are used to working at the theatre.

Compared to the big national houses like the RSC and National Theatre, however, time is very tight indeed. Rehearsal periods for a

main house large production are only about three weeks on average —
something to bear in mind when you hear those who work in the big
theatres saying they could do with ten instead of eight weeks. . . .
Because of this everything has to be done with speed and everybody
works very hard — sets, costumes, props, the lighting and sound, any
music, all have to be ready within a comparatively short period.

I visited the Crucible during its 1985/86 season, but the way the
theatre is organized and how it works is unlikely to change greatly in
the immediate future. The theatre had gone through a very hard time
before Clare Venables arrived in 1981. At one time it looked in danger
of losing its entire Arts Council grant. Not only did that not happen, it
was given the largest grant of any regional Rep in the Arts Council's
controversial Glory of the Garden document on funding in 1984 —
much to the rage and chagrin of many of its rivals.

It was not possible, practically, to talk to all of the 150 people who
make up the Crucible company but it is interesting to see what goes
into the running of a theatre like the Crucible and to note how times
have changed: no longer is it possible for instance to have just an
artistic director, however competent or talented, as the whole business
of finance needs a professional hand. Likewise with publicity — a few
posters and a piece in the local rag about the leading lady won't fill
enough seats to keep a theatre of this size in business, so marketing,
press and publicity are now a vital part of a regional Rep.

We will look first at the work of some of the administrative side of
the Crucible; then at the practical matters of production (it is
interesting to compare, say, stage management in Sheffield with stage
management at Stratford); ending with the director herself.

Geoffrey Rowe, the Crucible's administrator, became involved in that
side of things early. Reading English and Drama at Hull, he acted a
little but was 'the kind of student who organized shows and publicized
things, did deals, tried to raise money and took shows up to
Edinburgh. None of it was in a very grand way but one of the things I
did was to take a little company from the university to a little theatre
in London and organize the whole event, which was really a kind of
early training in this sort of job.'

The exterior and interior of the Crucible Theatre.

From university he went to Derby Playhouse as house manager and then administered the university theatre in Manchester. He learned a lot in both jobs, he says.

'I suppose you could say now that I'm the one who ties it all together. I have a finger in every pie. You have to be a bit of everything from an accountant to a diplomat but it's a curious job in this day and age because you have to be able to do in a small way the kind of work that would be given to a number of different people in a large organization. For instance, we couldn't afford a personnel manager or personnel department here; it's us. Then there are the legal, organizational, and financial ramifications as there are in any degree of artistic enterprise, and it's my job to ensure that that side is covered so the artistic side can carry on and the director can get things done.'

His job covers obtaining rights and licences, dealing with contracts, raising finance, employing staff and looking after them in the way of salaries and wages, their contracts of employment, health and safety. Actors are straightforward, he says, compared to, say, caterers! A big catering enterprise like that of the Crucible is a two-edged undertaking. It can make you a nice extra income to help subsidize your theatre, but if you get it wrong it can soon run up enormous losses.

A repertory theatre in a provincial city must keep its links with the local community. This is vital 'not least because we draw so much of our income from public money which includes the rates'. So part of his task is to develop good relations with the local council, encourage community arts, see how the theatre can participate in local events. At the same time there has to be a constant relationship with the Arts Council which provides the single biggest part of the theatre's funding.

He does not think the Crucible was merely lucky in doing so well out of the Glory of the Garden. A good deal of work went into producing the submission for more funds, work that involved most of the administrative side of the theatre over a considerable period of time. Some of that time went into 'getting the local authority on our side and making sure we were asking for something they would want'. This meant that there was an input from the city itself as to what they would like to see and what the city was prepared therefore to put extra funds towards. 'It's a very entrenched socialist area and very supportive to anything which is educational and it is in favour of cultural amenities which are available to everyone.' Having said that he points out that all finance at the Crucible is monitored with an eagle eye. The newly re-formed Theatre-in-Education team has meant more work again to find out what schools will expect from it.

Ensuring people can actually see shows easily is vital and that means a good box office. Anyone who has had to hang on for half an hour when ringing a commercial theatre in the West End of London, only to get a bored person on the other end who obviously could not care less, will understand how important this is. 'People want the phone answered promptly, they want to be able to book by credit card, they want speedy service. Running the box office and forward booking properly is a time-consuming business and obviously thee way forward is by computer.' (The Crucible has introduced a special 'Crucible card' for series booking which will be dealt with later.)

He has an input into what plays are to be done but only on a general and 'conversational' level, he says. He is around when the season is being discussed and can make suggestions. He goes to the theatre outside to see as much as he can, from the National to Ken Dodd. 'We can be discussing the season and someone will say we need a light comedy which is quite classy and it might be me, as it was last time, who said "what about *Present Laughter?*" I give that as an example but actually it didn't do very well. . . . But we all need people to bounce ideas off.'

It would be pleasant in some ways, he says, to have a permanent company but it is not really possible — you could hardly keep a full pantomime company on well into the New Year for instance. You certainly could not offer a season of nothing but large-cast plays with expensive sets and costumes. 'Our problem is not paying for stars — if you think they will bring the money in then you can probably afford one or two big names — it is a matter of raising the overall level of money paid so that you can have a substantial number of mature, middle-aged, experienced actors here and can offer them a decent wage. It's not the big national name for Hamlet, it's the good middle-ranking actors for Claudius and Polonius. You've got to try and tempt them out of London and that's quite difficult. As we don't have a permanent company another task is finding them places to stay. We have a lady who keeps a list of digs and keeps a note of what people say about them, whether they are good, indifferent or just plain awful. You can't expect people to work well if they have nowhere decent to stay.

'To sum up, I'd say the joy of my job was to enable the artistic policy, plans and schemes to be actually carried out.'

Bill Farr, the finance controller, came into the theatre from outside the theatre business all together. He has been a chartered accountant for fifteen years and arrived in Sheffield to work in a branch of a

Martin Duncan in *Present Laughter*.

national company. He took on the job, he says, when the theatre was in a terrible state and had reached an all time low. It was a challenge.

Since he arrived, he says, the theatre has actually made a small profit, which was his aim. The most important thing is to break even 'but it's even better if you can actually have a small surplus. It means we can liberate about £25,000 which we can then spend on capital refurbishment. We can't just rely on the city giving us more and more money every year. They did give us some capital money the last couple of years but you can't just expect it as of right.'

It usually takes about five attempts to get the overall budget right, he admits. The low risk part of the season is the first six months of the theatre's financial year — from March to September. The Crucible has become famous for its televised snooker, which takes place in April and fills the theatre. The snooker income is very important not only to the theatre but to the city — it is thought to bring about £1 million into Sheffield every year. In May and June there are studio shows, and it does not matter too much, he says, if they are sold out or only play to 30 per cent capacity: this can be covered, as the actual financial impact on the theatre is minimal. The cast is usually six but can be stretched to seven if necessary.

In August the entire theatre goes dark after a period when it has played host to some touring shows. It's from September that the real risks begin and just how successful the whole year will be financially is partly dependent on the popularity of the pantomime. The panto-mime should take between £100,000 and £150,000 at the box office 'so a slippage of ten per cent the wrong way is a substantial figure, a lot of money to have to try and make up during the remaining three months of the year. It would be ideal if we could start our financial year on 1 January then we could take all our financial risks at the beginning and adjust during the year. As it is the major risks come at the end of the season.

'By the time you reach November you are committed to what you are doing in February and March. It is very much a "flying by the seat of your pants" job. I have to prepare a budget with a lot of elasticity in it to enable the directors to do what they have planned, and so that if we do have a down turn at the box office they don't have to sack two or three actors or cut back drastically on sets and costumes. The other area of my job is to keep really tight financial controls on everything else such as catering — in fact to do all those boring things accountants are supposed to do.'

The average income when I visited the theatre was £2 million, half made up from grant-aid bodies (including the £611,000 from the Arts Council) and the rest from other sources — touring, lettings, contributions from visiting companies, catering and so on. The new Theatre-in-Education has been an added expense, not least because there is no box office take for it.

He takes part in the discussions over what plays should go on 'but the final responsibility lies, of course, with the artistic people. I don't think one should really intrude on the artistic policy. Clare describes what she wants to do and I work out the figures to the best of my ability, although there obviously has to be fine tuning as the year goes on. But if someone suggests a show and says the box office return will be about 45 per cent but I think it will only be 25 per cent then obviously I'll say. I will give the opinion, if you like, of the common man.'

James Woods is head of marketing. Marketing, press and publicity is essential to the whole enterprise and is finally being recognized as such in theatre companies. He read English and Drama at university and worked as an assistant and then deputy stage manager. It was while working at the Phoenix Theatre in Leicester that he became fascinated by the marketing and publicity side — in part because he was involved at one time with a company which just did not get much coverage at all. He wanted to find out why.

He is rightly cynical about how companies have, in the past, seen the role of the publicity person. 'There is the old fashioned method largely organized to please the company. You sent someone on ahead when you toured. They had three posters. One went up in the local caff, the other in the nearest pub and the third by the stage door. When the company got there they thought you'd done a wonderful job as everywhere they went they saw publicity for the show — they only went to the caff, the pub and the theatre. They couldn't understand why few people actually came to see them. The other extreme is the small company who has got the message and advertises for superman or superwoman — you know the kind of thing. They want someone to take complete control of all press coverage, design all the publicity material, see to its being printed and then distributed, go out and find an audience, raise the awareness of the community to the existence of the theatre, bring in extra money for finance, make sure there is saturation coverage if they tour. . . . you'd be unlikely to get someone like that for £50,000 and usually all they can afford, if they are lucky, is £5000.

'In a largish Rep like this it's a totally different ball game. Although the end product is artistic you are still marketing it and you must never forget how important it is. Just think, companies like ICI have

A Christmas pantomime, *Jack and the Beanstalk* (left to right): Bobby Knott, Maggie Carr, Don Cran.

enormous departments devoted to nothing else.' It might sound obvious, he says, but the first thing you have to find out is just who your audience is.

Sheffield is unlike any other major city, even Manchester and Liverpool, in that its middle-class population (those considered to be the most likely theatre-goers) is well below average. It is a working-class city with a university and a large polytechnic. So 3000 theatre-goers were surveyed. All they had to do was to give their names, addresses and postcode and these were sent to a specialist firm for analysis from which it was possible to deduce the main areas of the city from where the audience was drawn and what they did. This means that advertising, leaflets, postcards, brochures, put into the local freesheets, could be concentrated first on the areas where they were more likely to meet with a response.

It is also necessary to have a wide-ranging programme to cater for such an audience. 'The feminists and students, for instance, might never want to see anything in the main house, while those who enjoyed *Present Laughter* or *Carmen Jones* might never set foot in the studio. One marketing idea which has proved very successful is the Crucible Card, and during the first season it was offered the theatre sold nearly 2000. For £12 you can see every show. Unlike some series bookings you do not have to have the same day and the same seat in the same week of each month. You can literally come any time you want to. If, however, you find you have left it too late and cannot get in on any night then your money is refunded. This has meant that people are keen to get their money's-worth and will therefore see plays they might not have thought of going to see otherwise.

Then there is the more obvious kind of publicity too. Dealing with the local media, radio and newspapers, national papers when it seems there is a story, arranging for incoming actors and actresses, playwrights and personalities to give interviews to the media, ensuring there are adequate photocalls.

James thinks it is unfortunate the Crucible is the only theatre in Sheffield. 'In Newcastle, where I used to live, there are five and other community venues as well. That means the whole city is in the habit of theatregoing — you can see that when the RSC go up there for their six weeks' tour. The old Lyceum Theatre across the road has stood empty for years. It's a short-sighted policy of the council. If it could be

Marshall Ward and Yvonne Gidden in *Carmen Jones*.

opened up for touring companies, ballet, opera, plays, and so on it would actually help us, not take our audience away.'

To run a successful theatre today the two sides of marketing, finding your audience and promoting your season, must be done as professionally as possible. 'After all,' says James, 'in a way it is so much easier than selling anything else. Just take newspapers. Most of them like running features about people and about stage personalities — whether it is some TV star who is in Sheffield with her baby while she is in a play or whether it is a new young playwright with something radical to say. Think of the difference between that and, say, a company making ball bearings — they have to *pay* for every column inch that is printed. Theatres get their editorial publicity free.'

So the budget for the season is agreed and the director, in consultation with others, has decided what plays are to be done. Then what? Well, it is necessary to sort out if all the plays are available and it is even more necessary to have actors to put in them.

Casting for the season and researching rights and availability of plays is the responsibility of Nic Horsey. 'Casting', he says, 'obviously occupies most of my time. We have five directors and basically I'm on call for all of them. I'm their gofer (dog's-body). I'm always working on different time scales. For instance we've a show that goes into rehearsal in a fortnight's time and that still isn't finally cast; but I'm also casting *Carmen Jones*, which doesn't go into rehearsal for six months but for which I need a fairly large number of black actors. It's difficult to get a director to look very far ahead — especially six months ahead — when they are deep in what they are doing at the present moment.

'For a big show we usually book a room in London or Manchester and we'll be looking for two or three characters each day or one leading role if we have already seen a lot of people. After that it might be more convenient and relaxed to get the final people up here to talk to the director over a cup of coffee. There is something which has proved quite interesting. Obviously if you see a dozen people for a part you can only offer it to one of them, but again and again people we have seen for one show have stayed in the mind and we've picked them out weeks or even months later for another part in another show.

'Agents are beside themselves with joy when I send them a letter saying "is so-and-so in work at the moment?" I always keep the c.v. and a photograph on file of anyone we have found interesting. It works the other way, too. A director who auditioned a play here then went on to do a play in Leeds, 'cast two people he had not used at Sheffield but thought would be suitable for the next play.'

Since most of the acting profession spends its time resting, how you get cast is an all-consuming passion with most of them. Not all agents are helpful, says Nic. Some still talk about weekly Rep and not doing anything 'out of Town', meaning London, 'as if we were still living in the 1930s. In fact there is more theatre going on outside London than in. There are a lot of good commercial agents who are spot on, though. They attend degree presentation shows at drama schools as, indeed, do I. Good agents will pick up promising actors right there, with or without Equity cards, and push them for all their worth. Another innovation which has happened during the last couple of years and is really taking off is a kind of actors' co-operative agency. A group of them, say ten or twelve, sell themselves. They have an office with a manned phone, they do a brochure and those who are not working will man the office and push those who are out of work. Some agents take only a small percentage from young actors in provincial Rep but others are really extortioners. The benefit of the co-operatives is that they only take a small percentage, to pay for their running costs. They don't have to pay out for wages and expensive offices. There are a number of them now in London, Manchester and Birmingham and now we have one in Sheffield.'

Some hopefuls just write direct to the director, Clare Venables. 'A number of the people I've been seeing during the past weeks have written straight to Clare without any agent. She passes the letter on to me and I tell them basically what work we are doing this season. I might say that from their c.v. nothing that Clare is doing herself is suitable but I'll show it to either Mike or James who are also directing shows. There is a certain amount of P.R. in this job and quite rightly so. There should be someone who can deal directly and courteously with actors.

'If an actor writes and says why hasn't he or she heard anything since writing six months previously I write back and tell them that it is because nothing has come along for which I thought he/she would be suitable, but if it does I can promise his c.v. will be seen at the right time — and it is.'

The other half of the job is rights. 'We have to work well ahead. Some of the projects, if they come off, won't happen until next year or the year after. We find, especially with big musicals, that the reason they have not been performed for years and years is because the rights are owned by some smart New York lawyer or the rights have gone from the person who wrote it to a second cousin, or their children, or were bought by a holding company who have then been sold out or bankrupted, so I spent a lot of my time courting New York lawyers who don't really have any idea how British repertory theatre works. They think it is like American summer stock — a few people putting on a little show for four weeks in August. They imagine the Crucible Theatre in Sheffield is some kind of a shed or hut on a waste lot at the back of a factory with a cast of about six people.'

It took him a considerable while to get the rights of *Carmen Jones*. The problem when I saw him was that they had found themselves a wonderful Carmen 'but she's over six foot and that's proving really tough. Most tenors are only about four foot three. . . So you can see what a long, drawn-out and difficult business both getting hold of a play or musical and then casting it has become.'

Going back to those auditions. Are they fair? Do the Crucible management sit there like in the movies half way back in the darkened theatre saying 'next please'? 'You're thinking it's all like the auditions for the singing and dancing Hitlers in the film *The Producers*. No, on the whole today's directors don't like formal auditions and actors certainly don't because they very often don't really tell you what that actor can do. The main reason you ask for an audition piece is so that you can remember the tone of the voice. It's later, when you have a discussion and you find out something about them and how they've tackled what they've done, that you see how they might fit in with what you want. The way Clare and Mike and I work is basically a chat, a talk through someone's c.v. and then you get them to read. It's a much better way.'

And is there any truth in the old myth of the person who lands a leading role by good luck? 'It does happen. It happened here. We'd auditioned goodness knows how many girls to play Juliet and none were quite right. Then one night in the pub one of the electrics lads brought along his girl-friend who was just out of drama school and there she was, our Juliet . . . . Just what we'd been looking for.'

So you have chosen your show, it is budgeted for; if it is a new play or if the rights need to have been acquired this has been done and it has also been cast. What next?

The designer will have produced designs. A repertory theatre like the Crucible is more likely to have both sets and costumes designed by one person but this is not always the case. However, whether or not it is the same person, he or she will have produced a model to show what the set will look like. This is agreed with the director of the play and then the workshop sets about constructing it. The Crucible has nothing like the numbers of workshop staff as, say, the RSC but it is fortunate in having its own workshops in house and a staff permanently available.

John McCall is in charge of the workshop where the set is built. (You will find that most people who work backstage at the Crucible talk lovingly about the railway train in the theatre's extremely successful 1984 production of *The Railway Children*. It looked so real it convinced the audience, and it was remarkable as the picture shows.) John did not do any special art school training or course but had been in the RAF. After leaving the service he drifted for a while, he said, before ending up in the workshop at the Crucible 'just cutting things up'. He became more and more interested in the business of constructing sets and dealing with the materials involved, as he worked. 'I believe there is no better way to learn.' John and his small team of three or four make all the sets for the main house, studio and the Theatre-in-Education team.

It calls, he says, for a great deal of flexibility to deal with the varying types of set design and materials used and the limits imposed by where a play is to be performed. For example a Theatre-in-Education set will need to be easily erected in a school hall but must also be capable of being packed away and stowed in a van at the end of the day.

All kinds of materials are used — steel, fibreglass, timber, plastic, canvas. As steel is now cheaper than timber it is mainly used for the structure of the set; then it is clad in thin plywood to achieve the designer's effect. When I was there he was working on the set for *Macbeth* and working very hard. As in most main house Crucible shows the workshops only have from three to four weeks to produce sets, props and costumes. The steel framework had been constructed and the plywood was being cut. Large sheets of plastic were to be used to simulate stone. A good deal of time goes in simulating and breaking down. As Bill Lockwood said, it is rare that anything new looks right under stage lights and so it has to be treated to make it look natural. Likewise cheap material has to be made to look like the real thing so that the audience are fooled even when they sit as close to the stage as they do at the Crucible.

He had persuaded the designer in this case to give up the idea of steep, if dramatic, ramps in favour of flights of stairs. 'There is a good deal of compromise needed,' he says. 'Also you can be asked to do something which is just too expensive but we will always try and do what the designer wants if we are able to, given the time-scales involved. It is also necessary sometimes to point out possible hazards — nobody wants an actor to break his neck.'

The workshops work to a tight budget. Sometimes, says John, a show can seem cheap as all the materials are cheap — for example the plastic sheets used in *Macbeth* only cost £4 each — but the same show can require an enormous amount of labour and by the time you have added overtime and extra days worked then it is no longer a cheap show. 'For instance that train in *Railway Children* was cheap in materials but took a massive amount of work. We built it in here (the workshop is behind the stage) and it ran on to the stage from here. It was marvellous, though — you heard the audience gasp. Our job is to make something look like something else — we are the makers of illusion.'

Downstairs Neil Gidley is working on the props. Neil Gidley *is* the Props Department at the Crucible, only rarely does he have any assistance. He was working away surrounded by the kind of prize objects Bill Lockwood had in his office — yet another severed head, a large and foul rat, and an Aladdin's lamp. He did a BA in sculpture at Sheffield and then came to the Crucible as a scene painter. 'I just worked on this and that and gradually moved up until I helped the props man who was here at the time. Eventually he left and I took over.'

He makes, he says, everything that moves — furniture, weapons, masks, replicas of existing things such as fake food, severed limbs, heads (they all seem to love heads), statues, artifacts. . . just about anything. The modern materials are used to the utmost, fibreglass, polystyrene and other synthetics. You can use almost anything, he says. It's 'a case of if it looks right, use it!' All items are then fire-proofed with the required fire-proofing solutions.

He was working on shields for *Macbeth*. They were made up in fibreglass resin from a mould that he had made. 'Often it's the things you wouldn't think would be difficult that take the time. Few people going to the theatre realize that you don't just make an object. Very often you have to make the moulds and then casts from the moulds and it all takes up a good deal of time. Sometimes the simplest things are the worst.'

He also has to work very tightly to budget and 'I do try to do everything cheaply'. Properties are stored and used again where possible even if they have to be adapted second time round. One of the biggest projects on which he worked was that train. He and the set workshop worked off a scale drawing — the train was actually about

The train in *The Railway Children* – one of the theatre's most successful productions.

five-sixths real size — making the body out of plywood built on to a steel frame. The wheels were made of plywood and the train actually ran on wooden rails treated to look like steel. Neil made the funnels for the train among other things, one of which had to actually produce smoke. 'We were devoted to the train. It's in a pub somewhere now. We couldn't bear to dismantle it and we preferred it went to a good home.' He has also made, on request, three large dragons for a pantomime, a sarcophagus — the range is limitless.

The unpleasant rat had been made with a clockwork inside for a pantomime and the severed head was Macbeth's. 'It was rather difficult to do as he has a beard and I had to cast over it. I'm just about to add the hair and the beard to the cast. When they bring it in at the end it should look like him. I'll probably use paint for blood, though we do use property blood if we want it to drip.'

A prop maker certainly needs diverse skills. As you look around and see the goblets, shields, armour, weaponry, Aladdin's lamps, furniture which surround him you realize just how skilled a job it is. As I left the telephone rang and there was a brief conversation. He put it down. 'I've got to make a thumb in a hurry. A human thumb. I assume it's something to do with the witches. . . .'

Ann Robinson trained at Wimbledon School of Art and did their theatre design course. She had set her heart, she says, on working in the theatre from an early age. 'At the end of my last term at college I knocked on the door of the Crucible and started work as a dresser on *Chicago*.' She did odds and ends at Sheffield, freelanced in wardrobe departments elsewhere and ended up as an assistant cutter at Glyndebourne. I thought when I arrived there that I wouldn't actually have to *cut* anything. As an assistant in such a large organization I assumed a master cutter would cut a costume and then give it to me to tack together to pass on to the person making it up, but to my horror the first thing they did was give me the design for a 1765 brocade dress for the Countess in *Marriage of Figaro* along with yards of the most expensive silk brocade you can imagine. All I'd cut out before was a dressing-gown and a few skirts gathered on to waistbands. This one was full of pleats, it had great paniers. So I went away and sat in the toilets for ten minutes and thought about it. Then I took a deep breath and started in.

'When it came to the first fitting all it needed was something like half an inch taken in at the waist. I was very proud of it; it was an exquisite dress. I found it satisfactory to go through something I had been terrified of and find it worked and looked lovely. It looked beautiful on but then the singer was beautiful so that helped. That was the most satisfying garment I have ever made.'

By the time she arrived back at the Crucible she had had considerable experience and now, 'and it's very satisfactory', she is head of Wardrobe.

The Wardrobe too has only between three and four weeks for each show. The work required varies enormously from twenty-five people and several costumes each in a musical or pantomime to a two-hander in modern dress in the studio. She discusses with the designer what they want for each character and then draws up a costume list for the show, discusses choice of fabrics, finds out who needs a wig, who has quick changes, what can be used from existing stocks. From this list she works out how much the Wardrobe Department will need to spend, and if it is within the budget she goes straight ahead organizing shopping trips, ordering shoes and wigs, hats. Actors and actresses are measured and the rush begins.

The budget is all important and she has to stick to it whatever flights of fancy might inspire the designer. 'I can't let them go mad. I've a budget to think of and there's no question of letting them loose to spend thousands of pounds on a handful of outfits. This morning, for instance, we needed blouses and skirts for a modern show and I know how much I had to spend so that was fairly easily done in the city's chain stores. I've just started shopping for *Macbeth* and I have £2000 to do it on and I've worked out I've already spent £500.

'If it's a period show, say, with Tudor costumes, I talk to the cutters about how it should be cut to make sure they know what is needed for the right period and that they are following traditions exactly. We check up and research how it was done originally. If there is a special problem where, say, a costume has to come off in three seconds then we have to think about that while we're making it up. I then supervise them to make sure it is right. We're working like mad on *Macbeth* now and we've only two weeks in which to get it all done. That happened because the Theatre-in-Education show we did earlier took a lot longer than we had thought it would and a good deal of imagination and energy. It had large puppets that we had to cover and they were very detailed. It was a lot of work for such a show when we had a major production coming off too.'

With period costumes and costumes for a major show you have to be good at making something look like something else. 'I have to steer the designer away from the expensive brocade shops towards the furnishing department at John Lewis's. We hand-paint on plain silk, which can look very exotic — indeed it can look just as good, if not better, than what we would buy if we had more money to spend. We did *Romeo and Juliet* last year and I bought almost all the materials in Sheffield — although we usually buy in London. But this *Romeo* was set in the early 1900s with lots of light grey and black wools and as it was September the local shops were full of Viyellas and flannels so we were all right shopping here.'

The worst problem for Wardrobe is when a designer just does not seem to know what he or she is doing. For one Shakespeare play all the designer gave her was a box of crayons and a colouring book from the National Portrait Gallery and told her he wanted something like 'some of these. . . .'

For *Funny Girl* the problem was the sheer number of costumes, the chorus girls having eight or nine changes of costume and again it was a question of referring to the reference books. Men's suits had to be hired. 'To make one properly with all the tailoring was just too time-consuming. In fact, if you have someone making such a suit properly it would probably take them the entire production time for that show to make that one suit. So we concentrated on the clothes for the girls. Compared with this, *Macbeth* is relatively easy, largely a question of piecing together skins and trousers and shirts.' Coming up was the pantomime, which she enjoyed in 'a masochistic sort of way'. The wardrobe team expands from eight or nine to about twelve for that. 'It's quite a jolly thing to work on and it is so good working here because they are a nice friendly team and they're efficient too.

'I love to sort out the problems. Most of the time you are doing something you've never tackled before. I liked trying to make an actor look like an English sheepdog for Peter Pan. I like trying to recreate a period costume exactly as it would have looked at the time, so different to the kind of things we wear now. I like trying to get someone who is totally modern in appearance to look perfectly in period — to step back in time.'

Once a show gets into rehearsal proper then light and sound has to be worked out. Geoffrey Mersereau trained in summer stock in Canada but has worked in this country for many years. He worked on all kinds of shows while going through college ('no grants over there you know. . .') and drifted towards lighting, although it was not, he said, looked on as a career in those days. He found career prospects in Canada pretty restrictive and spent some time working with a lighting designer in New York before coming to Britain.

He and his two assistants are responsible for designing all the lighting for each show along with operating it and maintaining it. Related equipment includes things like smoke guns, pyrotechnic units

Cider with Rosie (left to right): Robin Sneller, Peter Biddle, John Ramm and Liz Stooke.

and individual lamps. Wherever possible all special items are made up within the department. There are, he says, over 300 stage-lights in the building, ranging from very simple 500 watt floodlights to 1000 watt compact source iodide follow-spots, all linked to a fully computerised lighting control in the main auditorium with 160 dimmers. There is a simpler set-up in the studio.

'Oddly enough lighting has not seen such enormous technical advances over the last few years as sound. It is very much as it was twenty years ago except that computers have become far more sophisticated. They have come within the reach of anybody as they can be brought off the shelf.' (Computers can still cause awful problems, and those who have worked in other theatres can tell hairy stories of what happens when you wipe a computer's memory clean by mistake at the start of a show, or what happens when it goes slightly wrong, jumps several cues, and then carries relentlessly on.)

The Crucible now has an extremely sophisticated computer 'and you would be hard put to drive it to its limit. We can produce the most complex lighting we are ever likely to need. In relation to everything else in the budget, lights are relatively cheap too. But an audience expects nowadays to see a very sophisticated show. They are used to good lighting on television and at the cinema. They expect standards at least as good when they come to the theatre. For example the famous train relied heavily on lighting to achieve its effect.'

When it finally appeared he said it was 'quite a moment'. One of the most difficult shows he had to do at the Crucible was *Peter Pan* because of the way the auditorium was constructed. With no proscenium stage it meant that Peter Pan and the Darling children had to fly out over the audience with nothing to hide the wires. 'You know the kids are all there looking for the wires. We did our best but I don't think we entirely succeeded in hiding them.' After that *Macbeth* is easy. 'This is about the tenth time I've done *Macbeth*. I've done it in French, in English, in modern dress, in all kinds of period costume. Fortunately I've had a gap so I don't mind having another go at it. When you are tied to the O and A-level syllabuses you know it will keep on coming round.

His own preference is 'original plays where you can start in right from scratch. That's very creative. Otherwise what is needed in this job is great flexibility, to be able to go from a small intimate modern show to an enormous musical or to the pantomime with all the special effects that requires.'

Tony Bird, who is in charge of sound, actually trained in lighting and then decided to make the switch to sound. He found the courses on offer for both lighting and sound, at least at the time he was training, pretty irrelevant for work in the real theatre. He learnt far more while actually working, he said, and this also included touring with rock bands and producing all the lighting effects and looking after the sound.

There is a two-man Sound Department and its responsibilities include all the usual recording and mixing of sound effects and music and a good deal else besides. A typical week in a production season means the sound men will have to research, record and compile sound effects for the forthcoming production or productions, while operating the sound equipment for the evening shows in the main house.

'On a creative level it's my responsibility to read the script, come up with the relevant sound design, be it for a musical or for a straight scene show, and then present my scheme to the director. It's very much a case of continual consultation after that. Things will be changed where I haven't seen eye-to-eye with the director. There is continual tape preparation and, if it is a musical, I will need to put a smaller version of the sound system into the rehearsal room for the cast. *Macbeth* is a medium-sized show and we'll be running about four stereo machines with composite effects that have been made up on an original track. We're also doing odd vocal effects which basically means taking a straight, ordinary untreated voice and then making it into a synthetic sound. It's rather like making a Dalek voice — that's for the witch scenes.'

Much use is made in sound departments today of synthesizers 'which means in theory we can recreate any sound that has ever been made. It wasn't so many years ago that the sort of equipment we are using here would only have been found in a first-class recording studio. If we can sample a sound we can recreate it. Basically we record it — it's pretty technical but trying to put it simply: we take a lump of sound and sample that lump and look at what it looks like electronically, and then you add the next lump on to it and the next lump and so on until you get the full sound you want which is then stored away in the synthesizer.'

At this point someone came and asked him for an owl's hoot for *Macbeth*. How do you distinguish between an owl's hoot and a screech? 'Well there is only one owl which hoots; all the others make different kinds of noises. We listen to the different types and then record the one we want. If we can't actually create what the director wants then we buy it, which can be a hit and miss affair. Take the owls. You need to know what time of day it is and how high it's flying and, of course, what kind of owl it is. But you can do a lot just by putting on a tape and speeding it up or slowing it down.'

He is obviously a man who loves his equipment and could always go on refining what he has, but he says he is lucky. Most theatres don't even have a separate Sound Department, just an electrical one where an engineer makes sound tapes. The Crucible therefore has a better finished product although the deadlines are very tight. 'We never have the six weeks or so rehearsal period of a West End show followed by two weeks of previews.'

As well as producing sounds the Sound Department is heavily involved with performances, especially with musicals. The theatre can generally run to a fifteen- or sixteen-piece orchestra or even more. 'When you get twenty people hammering away and you have a big brass section you've got to make sure the voices can be heard over the top. You can't ask a trumpeter to blow a note quietly. . . . The real trick is in turning the microphones on and off and you have to be very subtle.'

He too remembers the train with affection. 'As it was five-sixths lifesize it reached all the way from the front of the stage to the back door. We had all the appropriate noises and a complete sound system inside the train so that when it whistled or steamed you actually heard it just as if it was real. It was only on for a minute or so and we'd have four men pushing it hell for leather down the tracks from behind and the train would be puffing and screeching and the brakes would go on and the sparks would fly off the rails and the audience clapped and cheered. We even had the train take a bow. It came on with the cast at the end and had a quick toot on the whistle, puffed with steam and trundled off.'

The Crucible has special problems. There are only two stages of that kind in the country and the way it thrusts out into the audience makes the placing of speakers for sound difficult. But you could always go on improving sound, he says, as new equipment pours continually on the market. The equipment at the Crucible runs into tens of thousands of pounds.

'But at the end of the day, of course, however sophisticated your equipment, however carefully you have planned everything and however meticulous you are, it can still go wrong. We have all had the experience of coming up to the crunch part of a play when all the crucial lights have to come on and you press the button — and nothing happens. . . .'

Sharon Eva Degan in *The History of Tom Jones*.

The stage manager is responsible for the smooth running of the whole show. He or, in this case, she, co-ordinates all notes from rehearsals, liaises between the director and all other departments, looks after company welfare and acquires all the props which have to be bought in, borrowed or hired. Basic requirements, says Alison Fowler, the Crucible's stage manager, are dedication, determination, patience, diplomacy and a sense of humour. She trained at the Central School of Speech and Drama and started in two-weekly Rep as an assistant stage manager and then came to Sheffield as deputy stage manager.

One of her main responsibilities is to ensure that all the jobs being done by other people are actually being done. She is also in charge of ensuring that specific props work in a particular way so that there are no problems for the actors, and that they are got to the rehearsal room as soon as possible, to allow the actors the maximum amount of time to work with them. She has to sort out the fittings for wardrobe calls to ensure that rehearsals are as little interrupted as possible 'which is tricky with someone like Macbeth who is in almost every scene almost all of the time.'

She has to arrange wig fittings, choose spectacles, acquire all the small props. 'We don't have much money to spend. We comb jumble sales, junk shops, rarely antique shops, ordinary shops just looking for things at as basic a cost as possible. We have to try and get everything here in time for rehearsal if possible or, at the very least, well before the production week. Normally we have three weeks then we're straight into production. If everything runs behindhand and we don't know what props are needed until the director reaches the last two scenes, we can find ourselves with only four days to get the real items which will be needed on stage.

'If a show needs animals then I have to arrange getting one from a pet shop and checking out what is needed with the RSPCA. We've had rabbits, hamsters, guinea pigs but also a goat, a donkey, snakes, rats, chickens — all kinds of animals. Coming up to the pantomime you might need an animal and be making arrangements for that at the same time you are dealing with an enormous list of props. We work a forty-eight hour week and we are supposed to have two sessions off a week, either morning or afternoon; but if you've got a very long show in performance that can take up to twenty-four hours and it would only leave you another twenty-four to do everything for the next show.'

The Crucible works with a stage management team of three. Two might be working on setting up a show while a third is on the rehearsal for the next. 'The deputy stage manager is the person on the book who attends all the rehearsals and is the one who actually keeps

134

an eye on everything and send us out notes from that rehearsal. He or she enters all actors' moves on the script or "the Book" as it is called, so if an actor falls ill an understudy can be called in and can use the script to follow the moves. The DSM checks all the props required, the costumes, sound and lighting effects requested; and during the technical rehearsal, as has been explained elsewhere, all the sound, lighting and scene changes cues are marked on the same prompt script so that the DSM can cue the show both verbally and with the red and green light system. At the end of every performance the DSM makes out a report which includes the length of the show, times for each act, how sound and lighting has gone and any relevant remarks either artistic or technical.

'To be a good stage manager you have to keep your head when all about you are losing theirs whether or not they are blaming it on you. There is always the worry that an actor isn't going to turn up after a weekend or that he's missed a train and can't get here on time. We had one show and it got to the Monday and all the men's clothes had been sent to the cleaners. It wasn't until 7 p.m. that wardrobe realized they hadn't come back. At 7.30 p.m. there was still no sign of them. We rang and rang and couldn't get through for ages. When we did they told us their van had broken down and we had to send a taxi up there. They finally arrived at five minutes to eight. . . . By that time the cast were standing in the wings in their underwear. The cleaners should have told us right away, not left it until the actors arrived in wardrobe demanding their trousers.'

Her job, she thinks, is probably not sufficiently appreciated by the general public. 'I don't think they know what we do. They just think we are there to bring things on, they don't think where they come from — some vast and bottomless store where you can pick anything out! The one thing you haven't time to be is temperamental because you have far too many temperamental people around you. You've got to be the one in control and be calm about the whole thing and just get things done. It's being aware of people, keeping everyone happy, sorting things out — I find it a challenge.'

So we come to the directors. The theatre's director is Clare Venables. Her associate is Mike Kay. Clare took a first-class honours degree in Drama at Manchester University and was immediately employed as a lecturer in the same department. From there she went on to direct in regional theatres all over the country, including the Victoria Theatre, Stoke-on-Trent where she directed *Fanshen*, *Mother Courage* and *Macbeth*. She was assistant director at the Theatre Royal, Lincoln, for two years before becoming director for three and went from there to the Manchester Library and Forum Theatres occasionally playing parts — including St Joan, Portia and Marie Lloyd. After a period of freelancing she became director of the Theatre Royal Stratford East and arrived at the Crucible in 1981. She has also directed extensively abroad in Canada, America and India.

Mike Kay, too, had spent a period at the Stoke Vic where he learned to use Peter Cheeseman's methods of working and devising a play from documentary material. He has also worked extensively in Theatre-in-Education. For him, the jump at Sheffield has been to direct plays with set texts — such as *Macbeth* – in a large theatre with a large cast.

The two do however seem to understand and complement each other well. Clare says that when you run a theatre you are running a whole small society. She is motivated, she says, by her attempt to create a vision — albeit inside a capitalist society and within the constraints that imposes. 'You aim to create an organization where everybody can create according to their abilities and desires and that's at the whole root of theatre. It's not like an advertising agency or a baked beans factory. The theatre itself is the power of life to me and the ideal society where people can understand the processes which affect them communally.

'Essentially the idea is to create dynamic work which will change our, and the audience's, view of how and what we are. It must also include doing shows that allow us to escape from how we are as well and I think that is a very important part of our job. *Sweet Charity* is probably rather more than just straight escapism, more say than *Anything Goes*, but it is a very good example. It is also a celebration of certain skills. Any show which celebrates the ability of the same person to act, be funny, tap dance, sing, uses the gifts of the human being to the full is very attractive to me. I do truly believe that escapist theatre has got a very real, important, social conscience and fulfils a deep need. The escapist theatre of the Depression of the 1930s was really important.

'Pantomime is another example of that. It's a sort of folk memory of our cultural heritage and it brings in to the theatre a whole audience which might never come to see anything else.'

Of course, whatever philosophy lies behind the choice of season there are obvious limitations. It has to be worked out within the theatre's budget; it has to take into account the number of people (not only actors) that can be employed and consideration has to be given to what can be done in that particular building and in those particular auditoria. But with these reservations in mind the programme, says

The History of Tom Jones. Steven Pimlott (left), Sam Williams (right) and John Ramm (standing).

Clare, is then sorted out between herself and Mike with some input from others. 'It's a three-way process. Part comes from staring at the ceiling and looking for images and ideas that will, purely selfishly, stimulate me. That's important because if the director isn't turned on by the programme and wouldn't want to go and see the shows, then why the hell should anyone else?

'So that's the first stage. If I think I'd like to see a particular show it stays in my draft list. It usually ends up with about three pages of plays we would both like to do. This is then knocked down to a short list.' It is at this stage Mike puts in his bid and both agreed they were surprised at how successful his production of *Catch 22* had been. Clare admits she had never thought it would go, but he had wanted to direct it so much she had given him the go-ahead.

'I suppose you could say we don't actually do a "balanced" programme here as some Reps do. That suits me as we haven't got a balanced audience in Sheffield. We have a very small middle class and when we do middle-class plays the theatre is just not full. I wanted to do *Present Laughter* as I adore Noel Coward and we hadn't done anything like it for a long time, but it wasn't very successful — that kind of play just doesn't have a root in the audience here at all. They don't like Ayckbourn either, though I love him.

'The final process of drawing up a season therefore is to ask "will it go?" If we feel a play has a truly common root then we put it on in the main house. If we don't feel that but we do feel there is an audience for a less obvious choice then it goes into the studio. I keep a list of all the plays I'd like to do "one day" such as Strindberg's *Dream Play* but that wouldn't be possible here. It's too big for the studio — although I dream of the day when we have sufficient funds to cast a large play in the studio — and wouldn't go in the main house.'

She was obviously delighted with the recognition given to The Crucible in the Glory of the Garden document and the subsequent higher funding. 'There was no luck or good fortune in the result. That didn't enter into it. We had sweated over our presentation document for two years and it was finally realized anyway that the Crucible was grossly underfunded compared with, say, the Manchester Royal Exchange with only one auditorium. The Crucible is actually the biggest regional theatre.

'It must have been like a madhouse at the Arts Council when they were working out the logistics of the Glory of the Garden and seeing how they could distribute the money, but I think that even if we had presented the Crucible's case badly we would still have been relatively high on the list. As it was, we presented an excellently-argued case and they recognized its basic justice.'

Do Clare and Mike work in a similar way, I asked. Clare says she could not have an associate director with whom she did not have a basic sympathy. She had seen a good deal of his work before he came to Sheffield particularly in the field of Theatre-in-Education (TIE) and she liked it from every point of view. There is, she says, a big difference between them because he was very experienced in TIE and she was not. Her main experience had been in mainstream theatre and Mike had done very little. 'So we feed off each other. He comes into my rehearsals and gives me notes and I go into his and give him notes. We join in and I think it is very healthy even though it can sometimes be a trifle unnerving for the actors. But I don't believe in the notion of director as God.'

Mike feels this is the way to learn. 'For example there is a basic logistical problem for me personally. I am used to shows using between four and six actors, which last an hour or so and for which I have a three-to-four-and-a-half week rehearsal period. So I have had to get used to having, say, sixteen actors for plays which run for two-and-a-half or three hours and for which the rehearsal period is still only three to four weeks. What I've learned from Clare when she comes in is that I intellectualize too much — unfortunately that fits in with the pattern of training of British directors. They like to sit and talk about it. Clare likes to get on with it.'

Indeed she does. She does not think that acting 'is about talking. I think that the case is different with TIE: that does require a good deal of talking, it's crucial, which is why I admire good TIE work so much — it's so much more rooted in the real world. But when you are dealing with a set script and actually acting — that is en-acting an action — which is what acting is all about, then that isn't about talking at all, it is about doing. So my rehearsal periods are very active and we never stop doing things. Mike talks more. Neither is right, but a combination of both is getting somewhere nearer to what is right.'

Mike explained that he had been used to devising what was wanted during rehearsals and getting the play together so that when the actors got up for the first time they have all 'that body of knowledge and experience in devising their own text on which they can draw'. The problems with that method arise, Clare adds, when you try and devise Shakespeare. . . .

Mike smiled ruefully but said that for him the process involved encoding what you wanted to say within a series of meanings and images, so for a Shakespeare play he would need first to decode it and then reconstruct it, so to speak. Both emphasized that they did not think their way best but that after working together for some time they hoped a working process would be devised which used the best of both of them.

139

'The other thing to take into account', says Clare, 'is that when either of us directs a play we are not just the director of that particular play, we are directors of this building directing a play and this feeds both ways into what happens during rehearsals. The two are vested in each other because we run the theatre very personally, direct in our own personal ways and rehearse very personally because that's the way we want to operate our theatre. However, a guest director coming in — and we don't use many — has a different relationship with the actors because all that he is committed to during the period he is directing is the actors and the text, whereas we are committed to the whole philosophy of the Crucible. We are responsible for what we generate inside the building and also communicate outside it and we have to have our antennae searching out what is happening in the world as well as what is happening in the building. It is a two-way process for us. It comes right down to the most basic things like a director dealing with an actor's tantrum during rehearsal. They are simply dealing with one actor. We are having to put it in the context of how we run the theatre as a whole.'

The theatre, they say, is run on a very open basis. There are firm rules at the root of it which are to do with giving everyone their own space and their respecting the rules of the institution. That is really important to both of them. 'That's why I keep going back to the idea of this theatre as a small society. I don't want to create things over people's dead bodies. I would rather have a play that isn't going to win every award under the sun but in which everybody is functioning to the best of their ability. That means making certain ground rules before you start. You can see a fine piece of creative work but I think it is rather chilling if it has to be done at the expense of the human soul. I'm not prepared to do that, to say that everything must be sacrificed to a certain ideal, because in the end people are more important than art. Art is only a reflection of how important people are. I've never admired directors who trample on actors. That's really about power, not about creating something.' Both say firmly that their practice of keeping an eye on each other's rehearsals helps prevent this. 'We remind each other', Mike says, 'that at the end of the day it's only a play.'

What comes across most strongly is how enthusiastic both are for their work and the work of their theatre, and this was reflected in the attitudes of all those who worked at the Crucible during the time I was there, whether in the coffee bar, wardrobe, workshop or on stage. Clare says she feels they are lucky to do what they do. 'I think that the people who have the most difficulties in this creative world are writers because they are the most tender of all the creative people around. We are only the secondary creators. For writers it is a terribly solitary world and that, in a way, is the most difficult thing for any society to take on board. . . .'

At seven o'clock the Crucible Theatre begins to run up to the evening show. It is the magic 'half' called out over the tannoy. The actors are making up in the dressing-rooms, the stage management is making sure props and scenery are right, the deputy stage manager is ready to take up his position to see the show through, lighting and electrics are ready to go, and from the loudspeakers comes the sound of the audience settling into the auditorium. Five minutes before 'curtain up' (although the Crucible has no physical curtain) the voice comes over the tannoy telling people to take their seats please as the show is about to commence in five minutes. The countdown starts, the audience noise rises higher and higher and suddenly music plays and it becomes quite, quite quiet.

Clare Venables looks elated. 'This is the real buzz for me, the real high. That wonderful moment, that feeling of anticipation when that voice comes over the tannoy telling people to take their seats, the noise and then the silence as the show begins. That's why I've never wanted to do television. I don't want to communicate to a thousand separate people sitting in their own individual homes. I want to get out and communicate to a thousand live people out there together in this theatre at a particular moment in time. That's what it's all about.'

And so the play begins.